Writing Handbooks

Writing Poetry

John Whitworth

A & C Black • London

First published 2001
A & C Black (Publishers) Limited
37 Soho Square, London W1D 3QZ

© 2001 John Whitworth

ISBN 0–7136–5822–3

A CIP catalogue record for this book is available
from the British Library.

Typeset in 10 on 12 pt Sabon
Printed and bound in Great Britain by
Creative Print and Design (Wales), Ebbw Vale

Contents

1. Poetry and Myself

Who are you?
I am a poet.
What do you do?
I write poems.
What are poems?
The things I write.
Who are you?
I am a poet.

Why do you do it?

You write poems. Or at least you want to write them. Why? It can't be the money because there isn't any, or at least not much and I expect you knew that. Fame, then? I've been on television (late at night when nobody is watching), and on radio too, but no heads turn when I walk down the street. I once talked about poetry to a hall full of French schoolchildren – someone in the question-and-answer session said that it was obviously an absorbing hobby. But it isn't a hobby: poetry is my life.

Philip Larkin said he wrote poems to preserve his experiences. Not for himself – he had diaries for that – but for other people. Poems are part of the memory of the human race. But, to become part of memory, a poem has to be memor*able*. How? For Ted Hughes it was the *sound* that did it – the rhymes and the rhythms he first found in Kipling's long-lined poems with an insistent beat. Like 'Mandalay':

> Ship me somewhere east of Suez where the best is like the worst,
> Where there ain't no Ten Commandments and a man can raise a
> thirst.

Hughes was 14 when bitten by the poetry bug. For John Betjeman it happened as soon as he could read, and for Dylan Thomas

1

(another sound man), before that. I read 'The Ancient Mariner' at school when I was 12:

> Within the shadow of the ship
> I watched the water snakes
> They moved in tracks of shining white
> And, when they reared, the elvish light
> Fell off in hoary flakes.

It was the way the long middle lines rhymed, and perhaps it was the word 'elvish' – I learned that verse and others by heart, though I didn't have to. We 'did' *The Merchant of Venice* and I recited this – unsure what some of it meant:

> Look how the floor of heaven
> Is thick inlaid with patens of bright gold.
> There's not the smallest orb which thou behold'st
> But in his motion like an angel sings,
> Still quiring to the young-eyed cherubins;
> Such harmony is in immortal souls,
> But while this muddy vesture of decay
> Doth grossly close it in, we cannot hear it.

And then there were the Scottish ballads – it was, after all, a Scottish school:

> The cock doth craw, the day doth daw,
> The channerin worm doth chide:
> Gin we be missed out o our place,
> A sair pain we maun bide

What is 'channerin'? I didn't know. (Actually it means 'grumbling', and is connected with that other splendid Scots word 'chuntering'.) An older boy did the whole of 'Tam o' Shanter' on Burns Night. I chanted bits like magic charms (to myself, I wasn't loopy) on my windy, rainy journey to school of a morning:

> But pleasures are like poppies spread:
> You seize the flower, its bloom is shed;
> Or like the snow falls on the river,
> A moment white – then melts for ever.

There was the marvellous, sonorous Richard Burton on the record of Dylan Thomas' *Under Milk Wood*: 'The sloe-black, crow-black night!' How did you do that? Could I do it too? I was a slow starter; I didn't write poems then (it wasn't that sort of school) and didn't write a *good* poem until I was nearly 30. In between times I toyed with an actor's life. 'Still doing murderers and brothel-keepers, John?' said a friend breezily at what turned out to be my last play. If I couldn't *say* it for a living, then I would have to *write* it. I shall go on doing so until I die. If I can. It doesn't always happen – Larkin ran out of poems and it caused him great distress of mind.

And you? Did a voice tell you, as it told Betjeman? Is that voice enough? The New Zealand writer, Janet Frame, says in her auto-biography:

> There is also the frightening knowledge that the desire to write, the enjoyment of writing, has little correlation with talent. Might I not, after all, be deluding myself like other patients I had seen in hospital, one in particular, a harmless young woman who quietly sat in the admission ward day after day writing her 'book' because she wanted to be a writer, and her book, on examination, revealing pages and pages of pencilled O-O-O-O-O-O-O-O. Or was that the new form of communication?

That *is* a frightening thought. I have it when my poems come back, as they did this morning, with a dismissive note. If you didn't have the desire to write then you wouldn't be reading this book. If you didn't have Janet Frame's fear that your writing was worthless, then you probably wouldn't be reading this book either. Can writing be *learned*? From a *book*?

Can writing be learned?

Between train-spotting and poetry, I played cricket. I read every 'How To' book I could borrow – Don Bradman's, Denis Compton's, Trevor Bailey's. I spent hours in the nets. Alas – I should have listened to the old cricket pro:

> Son, this is the whole *enchilada*:
> All the books and the coaching are...*nada*.
> The only sure way
> To improve on your play
> Is to hit it A BLOODY SIGHT HARDER!

But I *am* an old poetry pro. I know 'po-biz'. I can tell you about technique. I can explain how the market works. I am a mine of useful historical information. However, I can't make you a poet; *you* have to hit it a bloody sight harder. I did go on playing cricket, by the way: for the Second XI, for my college, for a really terrible club belonging to a firm for which I never worked and that never won a match.

Isn't poetry run by a clique?

The poetry world is full of backscratching and backbiting. Talent does not rise effortlessly, and rewards do not always go to the most deserving. In this, the poetry world is much like those other worlds – academic, political, business, etc. Nevertheless, in the long run it is better to be talented than to know the right people and pull the right strings. If you have the talent, the will and the patience, success is yours – probably.

Perhaps you are already hurling this book to the floor. Perhaps, like Janet Frame, you are very doubtful that you do have talent. If writers were confident, extrovert and outgoing they would probably not be writers. Larkin, with as much talent as any other poet in the last 50 years, was once asked if he had any particular problems as a writer. With his usual Eeyoreish moroseness, he answered: 'Just not being very good.' He meant it. By the standards he set himself – the highest – he believed that he was not very good.

But he *was* good; he just thought he might not be, measured by the highest standards – and what other standards matter? If practice does not necessarily make perfect, it certainly makes better. Weedy cricketers can take up body-building. This is a mind-building course for poets. Or word-building.

One more thing. I wrote this. Parts of it may seem to you to be mistaken, trivial, or just uninteresting. If so, then either I have written it wrong, or you are reading it wrong. But don't believe everything I say, and don't suppose there is nothing else to say, either. At the back there is a list of other books you might want to read. Most important are the books of poems – if you do not like *reading* poetry then you will never be a poet. But if you do, if you feel you would give a great deal to produce something like that – like Thomas Hardy or Tony Harrison, like Emily Brontë or Elizabeth Bishop – like but different, different because it is yours, then read on.

4

Exercise 1: The 50-word poem

There are many exercises in this book. Poetry is like most things – the more you do it, the better you get. Try this. Write something, anything, but exactly 50 words long, no more, no less.

> A radio is playing in a North London suburban street. A boy, about ten or eleven, drags his toes through the fallen leaves. Horse chestnut leaves, sycamore leaves, beech, lime, plane leaves – all the leaves proper to the pleasant tree-lined avenues of such quiet North London streets in October. It is 1951.

So far, so good. Except that's 52 words. What shall I cut? Perhaps 'or eleven'? No, I need that. I could write 'such streets in October'? But now the word count is 49. Do I add another tree? Rowan perhaps – they have rowan trees in streets like that. You see, already, with one very simple constraint – the 50-word limit – I am led into all sorts of editorial decisions. And poems are like that, the formal element constantly leading one to visions and revisions. It is the part of writing I like best.

Now, if you have successfully produced exactly 50 words, divide it into lines in any way that seems good. There is no rhyme or metre so that will not help you. What will you do? You might do this.

> A radio is playing
> in a North London
> suburban street.
> A boy, about ten say,
> drags his toes through the fallen leaves.
> Horse chestnut leaves, sycamore leaves,
> beech, lime, plane leaves –
> all the leaves proper
> to the pleasant avenues
> of such quiet North London streets in October.
> It is 1951

The lines follow speech patterns. Rather dull perhaps? What about this?

A radio is playing in a North
London suburban street. A
boy, about ten say, drags
his toes through the fallen
leaves. Horse chestnut
leaves, sycamore
leaves, beech, lime, plane
leaves – all the leaves proper
to the pleasant avenues of
such quiet North London
streets
in
October.
(It is 1951.)

Better? Worse? The problem with such 'free verse', as it is called, is that there is no agreed standard of comparison. But is this *truly* a problem? Are we afraid of freedom? Should we be?

2. What is Poetry?

I am a poet. Not a sentence I often use. It sounds pretentious – isn't 'poet' a title *other* people give you? Nevertheless, I *am* a poet. I give readings in draughty halls and windowless back rooms; I send poems off with an sae (stamped addressed envelope) to literary magazines; I judge competitions; I enter them too, and occasionally win money prizes – grumbling privately, incessantly, that the money is not more. I read what other poets write, with envy, astonishment, admiration, surprise, annoyance. I write poetry. What exactly is it that I write?

> BOSWELL: What is poetry?
> JOHNSON: Why, Sir, it is far easier to say what it is not.

Most of us are of Johnson's opinion. We know it when we see it but we can't describe it. Let us try the *Oxford English Dictionary*, the one you read with a magnifying glass. It says poetry is 'composition in verse or metrical language' which is 'the expression of beautiful or elevated thought, imagination or feeling'. Obviously true of some poems – Keats' 'Ode to a Nightingale', for instance – but not all verse is poetry, as Johnson himself pointed out with this quatrain (a quatrain is a four-line verse):

> I put my hat upon my head
> And walked into the Strand,
> And there I met another man
> With *his* hat in his hand.

Not all verse is poetry and, conversely, not all poems are verse. Some hardly seem to be the expression of beautiful and elevated thought, either:

Detail

Doc, I bin lookin' for you
I owe you two bucks.

How you doin'?

Fine. When I get it
I'll bring it up to you.

William Carlos Williams, who wrote that, is in all the anthologies and 'Detail' is typical of his work. Not a beautiful and elevated thought – and it doesn't rhyme or scan either. Is it really a poem? Charlie Brown asks, 'How do you know which poems to like?' Lucy answers, 'Somebody tells you.' So I am telling you: 'Detail' is a poem.

You don't have to like the poetry of William Carlos Williams. You don't have to like the poetry of that other William, either: Tolstoy thought *King Lear* was rubbish and said so. You *can* prefer some poets to others – all criticism is, at bottom, a matter of opinion. Yet when this rule is applied elsewhere (to politics, say) then some opinions are obviously better than others. An infant's view of Tony Blair may be cute, but it lacks political grasp; a child doesn't know enough, is not informed enough and doesn't care enough about politics.

So, unless you want to stay a poetic infant all your life – and some do – you need to know what Carlos Williams thought he was up to. You can still dislike it but it will be *informed* dislike. What you can't do is to ignore it, to pretend it never happened. You can't write like Keats because we don't live in Keats' world any more. Or you can, but it will be a *pastiche*, an imitation of the style of someone else. 'The Ancient Mariner' *began* as a pastiche of an old ballad, right down to the 'olde worlde' spelling (*see also* Kit Wright's 'George Herbert's Other Self in Africa' in Chapter 5). But why write like Keats? Keats did that supremely well. Why not write like yourself?

Writing like Keats

> St Agnes Eve – Ah, bitter chill it was!
> The owl – for all his feathers – was a-cold;
> The hare limp'd trembling through the frozen grass,
> And silent was the flock in woolly fold;
> Numb were the Beadsman's fingers, while he told
> His rosary, and while his frosted breath,
> Like pious incense from a censer old,
> Seem'd taking flight for heaven, without a death,
> Past the sweet Virgin's picture, while his prayer he saith.

This is the first *stanza* (the technical word for what many call a verse) of 'The Eve of Saint Agnes'. Not many poems do I like better – to employ a Keatsian inversion. But there are things Keats does, mannerisms he has, which are not the stuff of poetry now. They are of his age.

We would not write 'a-cold' nowadays, nor 'saith' instead of said. These were *archaisms* (old, outdated language) in Keats' own day – people did not speak or write like that, even in poems. We would not speak of a 'woolly fold': that is what is called a *transferred epithet* – the fold is not woolly, it is the sheep within that are so. We would not write 'limp'd' and 'seem'd' instead of 'limped' and 'seemed' – Keats does that to differentiate between limp'd (one syllable) and limped (two syllables), a distinction it is not open to us to make. We would not use inversions of the natural word order, or at least not so many: 'bitter chill it was', 'silent was the flock', 'numb were the Beadsman's fingers', 'his prayer he saith'.

Keats does these things because he is writing in the early 19th century and there was a particular *diction* (way of speaking) proper to poetry then. It was this diction Wordsworth was reacting against when he said that poetry should be written in 'language such as men do use'. Yet he himself wrote, in his 'Sonnet Written on Westminster Bridge':

> This city now doth like a garment wear
> The beauty of the morning

The archaic 'doth' and the inversion 'like a garment wear' certainly did not constitute language such as men do use. I'm not sure about 'garment'; it has a Biblical feel and yet it turned up in very un-Biblical places like garment factories. What I am saying is that even Wordsworth used the prevailing poetic diction. We do not. The flight from it had already gathered pace when Lewis Carroll wrote:

> 'For instance, if I wished, Sir,
>   Of mutton pies to tell,
> Should I say, "dreams of fleecy flocks
>   Pent in a wheaten cell"?'
> 'Why yes' the old man said: 'that phrase
>   Would answer very well.'

Poets now generally avoid archaisms, inversions of the natural word-order and 'poetic' versions of words (o'er for over, thorough for through) which are shorter or longer for the sake of the *metre* (*see* Chapter 8). They are freer with the metre too, and when they do rhyme – not as often as they once did, perhaps – they may use near-rhymes (round/send, escaped/scooped). Not all poets allow themselves these liberties – Vernon Scannell grumbles in today's paper that those making use of traditional metre and rhyme should do so consistently, quoting Thomas Hood: 'A shilling is a shilling and a bad shilling is no shilling at all.' Personally, I think rhyming in English is quite tricky if we disallow inversions in natural word-order, and a little loosening up of the rules elsewhere is probably a good idea. *See* Chapter 11 for a fuller discussion of this.

In some ways then, modern poets allow themselves more freedom than Keats ever did, but in other ways less. Poetry remains about as difficult to write; it is just that its fashions have changed. Why should that surprise us? Look at the clothes Keats wore, and remember that his father probably wore a wig. What about the names of our own great-grandparents – when will Percy, Edith, Cedric and Charity come round again? There are fashions in literature as in everything else. 'English must be kept up', as Keats himself said. Or, in the words of the modernist Ezra Pound, 80 years ago, we need to 'make it new'. Though we won't write like him either. 'What hast thou, O my soul, with paradise?' No, we will not write like that.

But I can't help thinking of Thomas Lovell Beddoes, Keats' contemporary, who wrote like Shakespeare – for all the world as if the previous two centuries had not happened. Nearer our own time, John Betjeman ignored the Modernist revolution and wrote like an Edwardian – or he did as far as the *forms* of his poems are concerned; his *content* is another matter. Many poets and critics still cannot accept that Betjeman was serious or could possibly be any good. But am *I* saying that Beddoes and Betjeman are no good? No, I am not even saying that they would have been better if they had been more up-to-date. The point is that Betjeman at least was not ignorant of what he rejected, and neither should you be.

Back to our dictionaries. There are two further *OED* definitions, a sign that even the dictionary-writers have trouble. These say that poetry is what poets write – a neatly circular argument that I put into the verse right at the beginning of this book. So what are poets?

What are poets?

'Poets are the unacknowledged legislators of mankind,' said Shelley, never one to understate his case. He certainly wanted to be a legislator as well as a poet; he, like Byron – and unlike Keats – was of the class born to rule. He wrote violent political pamphlets and stuffed them clandestinely into the backs of rich women's dresses. When that failed he attached them (the pamphlets, not the women) to hot air balloons and released them over the Bristol Channel. He also wrote political poems:

> I met murder on the way –
> He had a mask like Castlereagh –
> Very smooth he looked, yet grim:
> Seven bloodhounds followed him:
>
> All were fat; and well they might
> Be in admirable plight,
> For one by one, and two by two,
> He tossed them human hearts to chew
> Which from his wide cloak he drew.

That is from 'The Mask of Anarchy' and Shelley never wrote better. However, though poor Lord Castlereagh (the Foreign Secretary) blew his brains out, it was not Shelley's poetry but his own depression that led him to do so. WH Auden, very political in his younger, communist days, came to the conclusion that poetry never made any direct difference at all to the world of affairs. Milton – perhaps the most political poet who ever lived, and himself a man of power during his time as Cromwell's Secretary – wrote political pamphlets like Shelley, and, like Shelley, he wrote them *in prose*. The Chinese poet Lao-tzu, disappointed in his political ambitions, made his poems into paper boats and sent them down the Yangtse river, supposing that as good and efficacious a method of publication as any other. The truth is as Auden said, but it is not the whole truth. Poems do make a difference, they do change people's lives (they changed mine) but not directly, not like bombs and speeches.

Someone once told TS Eliot, 'I am a poet.' 'You mean,' said Eliot crushingly, 'that you write verse.' Poet is indeed a title you must earn. Meanwhile, think of yourself as someone who writes, or is trying to write, poems.

Why? why? why?

- Why is 'Modern Poetry' so difficult?
- Why isn't it in metre or rhyme?
- Why is it about unpoetic things?
- Why is it like chopped-up prose?
- Why does nobody read it except other poets?

These are not silly questions. Larkin's reputation is in a dip at the moment, mostly because of his unfashionable political opinions – he admired Margaret Thatcher and even dreamed of her. Despite this he remains, in my opinion, the finest English poet since the War. And he worried about modern poetry. More than 40 years ago he wrote this:

> At bottom poetry, like all art, is inextricably bound up with giving pleasure, and if a poet loses his pleasure-seeking audience he has lost the only audience worth having.

I think that is profoundly true. Can poetry have a mass audience? Is John Hegley a poet? Sometimes. Are Beatles lyrics poetry? Cole Porter? Bob Dylan? Often.

Good poets can write bad poetry

WB Yeats was a fine poet. 'The Lake Isle of Innisfree' is possibly his best-known poem, once publicly recited in unison by 100 boy scouts. Or was it 1000? But not everybody likes it. Another fine poet, Robert Graves, remarked acidly that he supposed the lines:

> And I shall have some Peace there, for Peace comes dropping slow,
> Dropping from the veils of Morning to where the cricket sings

meant that Peace came down the chimney every morning. He also said that 'the bee-loud glade' sounded like a mealy-mouthed newspaper report – d . . . you and your b . . . piano and the b . . . loud noises you make on it! Graves thought 'The Lake Isle of Innisfree' was a bad poem. Good poets can write bad poems: some marvellously bad poetry has been written by some marvellously good poets. All of us live with failure.

> My ear is open, like a hungry shark,
> To catch the tunings of a voice divine.
>
> The beetle loves his unpretending track.
> The snail the house he carries on his back,
> The far-fetched worm with pleasure would disown
> The bed we give him, though of softest down.
>
> This piteous news, so much it shocked her,
> She quite forgot to send the Doctor.
>
> As if this earth in fast, thick pants were breathing
>
> He suddenly dropped dead of heart disease
>
> From Gloucester church it flew afar –
> The style called Perpendicular –
> To Winton and to Westminster
> It ranged and grew still beautifuller . . .

These lines are – in order – by Keats, Wordsworth (twice!), Coleridge, Tennyson and Hardy. Perhaps one needs the confidence of greatness to be quite as bad as that. No, of course one doesn't: William McGonagall was, famously, as bad as that *all the time*:

Beautiful town of Montrose, I will now commence my lay,
And I will write in praise of thee without dismay,
And in spite of all your foes,
I will venture to call thee Bonnie Montrose.
Your beautiful chain bridge is magnificent to be seen,
Spanning the river Esk, a beautiful tidal stream.
Which abounds with trout and salmon,
Which can be had for the catching without any gammon.

I can do that. This is from 'The Crocodile':

Be not deceived by his smile
For his black heart is full of bile.
As soon as look at you
He will bite you in two.
Do not wonder
If he bites you asunder.
You will not laugh
As he bites you in half.
Yes, your pleas will be in vain.
He will bite you in twain.
For that is his style.
It is the nature of the crocodile.

Such stuff is called *doggerel*. It rhymes but does not obey any rules of metre. It can have a pleasant comic effect, which McGonagall did not intend but I did.

Why be a poet?

Remember what Betjeman said: that he wanted to be a poet as soon as he could read and write. Why? Partly to escape the family firm. As a child I knew I didn't want to work in an office because that was what my father did. Poetry can be a romantic option. But journalism might be more so, as the poet Gavin Ewart thought. Why a poet? Part of the answer is that you do not choose poetry; poetry chooses you.

My urge was to encase in rhythm and rhyme
The things I saw and felt (I could not *think*).

Betjeman again – the things he saw and felt. Encase them in rhythm and rhyme. Stop them from fading away. Poets have a strong sense of the evanescence of experience, the now-you-see-it, now-you-don't quality. Others feel that too, and they do other things; but poems *are* a way of hanging on to something. Larkin again:

> I came to the conclusion that to write a poem was to construct a verbal device that would preserve an experience indefinitely by reproducing it in whoever read the poem.

Preserving experience is hard and doesn't leave too much time for anything else. Most poets live uneventful lives. Hopkins, Larkin and McGough have, among many others, grumbled in verse about the uneventfulness of it all. Poetry is vicarious experience.

Exercise 2: Doggerel

Write a poem in McGonagallese doggerel – 10 or 12 lines and make them bad. Why am I asking you to do this? Because I want you to free yourself from the parrot-critic perched on your shoulder who has probably killed more poetry than ever booze or LSD did. I remember a friend at university showing me his poetry. I thought it was terrible but I kept my mouth shut because I was fond of him and because my own poems were rubbish of a more pretentious kind. I wonder now just how bad his poems were, or if their badness had a kind of goodness inextricably woven into them.

3. Modernism, Postmodernism and All That

I hear voices: 'I don't like Modern Art, Modern Architecture, Modern Education, Modern Fashion, Modern Girls, Modern Poetry!' One of them belongs to me – at least some of the time. I'm a natural curmudgeon; what else would you expect? But if it's poetry you are talking about, are you sure it's modern poetry that you mean and not Modernist poetry? Because there is a difference.

Modern or Modernist?

Modernism isn't modern any more – Dorothy L Sayers and GK Chesterton poked fun at it 80 years ago in the 1920s. Poems by Philip Larkin or Wendy Cope (which rhyme and scan and do a lot of the things that Keats' poems did) are modern, though emphatically not Modernist – in fact they are reacting against Modernism, which is the name of a movement in the history of Art.

Modernism

The Modernist movement began around 1914. Listen to Tchaikovsky's music for 'Swan Lake' (1876), and then to 'The Rite of Spring' (1913): you can *hear* Modernism, and so could the rioting audience at the first performance of Stravinsky's ballet. Look at a painting by Burne-Jones and then at one by Matisse: you can *see* Modernism. Sir Alfred Munnings, President of the Royal Academy in the 1940s and a 'dab hand' at painting racehorses, didn't like it.

> Sir Alfred Munnings, P R A,
> Roundly condemns Matisse
> Who does not paint like (shall we say?)
> Sir Alfred Munnings, P R A,
> In strong approval horses neigh:

16

Loud cackle human geese.
Sir Alfred Munnings, P R A,
Roundly condemns Matisse

Alan M Laing wrote that; it's a *triolet* (*see* Chapter 14).

Modernist poetry

'Peace upon earth!' was said. We sing it,
And pay a million priests to bring it.
After two thousand years of mass
We've got as far as poison gas.

This poem by Hardy – 'Christmas 1924' – belongs, in its technique, to the world of the previous century. Now look at poem #1
by EE Cummings. He usually signed his name entirely in lower
case which was one of Modernism's tricks, out of fashion now
(and none too soon according to some).

l(a

le
af
fa

ll

s)
one
l

iness

Though it looks odd, this is not a difficult poem. It falls down the
page as a leaf falls, with the fall of the leaf symbolising loneliness.
The word 'one' is included in l(one)liness. All those 'l's are leaves
falling. And so on. Not difficult, but Modernist. Hardy's rhymes
and metres could have been employed by Keats, even by Shakespeare; they are part of a tradition. Cummings, eschewing rhyme,
metre, spelling and capital letters, is 'making it new' in that phrase
of Ezra Pound's.

Not as new as all that, though. In the 17th century, George

Herbert wrote poems shaped like wings and altars; contemporaries did pillars and crosses. A (Modernist?) poem wriggles down the pages of *Alice in Wonderland*.

Nevertheless, Modernism *did* make a difference. One version of that difference, articulated vigorously by Ezra Pound, was that something was wrong with Art at the end of the 19th century and that Modernism fixed it.

> The common verse in Britain from 1890 was a horrible agglomerate compost . . . a doughy mess of third-hand Keats, Wordsworth, heaven knows what, fourth-hand Elizabethan sonority, blunted, half-melted, lumpy.

After the Victorian 'Lawn' Tennyson (beautiful surface, no 'natural' life) came the Edwardians and the Georgians, twits with posh first names like Rupert and Ralph and risible second names like Drinkwater and de la Mare, and they wrote Tory-tweedy poems about moonlight and fox-hunting in the yokel-infested countryside using outmoded language like 'whither' and 'silvery' and 'dim'. This slashing interpretation of literary history was still prevalent when I was young in the 1960s. A counter-version is suggested in sprightly fashion by Larkin in his celebrated introduction to *All That Jazz*:

> The term 'modern', when applied to art, has a more than chronological meaning: it denotes a quality of irresponsibility peculiar to this century, known sometimes as modernism ... [whose] two principal themes are mystification and outrage.

He may be on to something, though a 'quality of irresponsibility' was not peculiar to the 20th century. This is from 'Wind' by Sidney Dobell, one of the 'Spasmodic' school of poets in the 1850s.

> Oh the wold, the wold,
> Oh the wold, the wold!
> Oh the winter stark,
> Oh the level dark,
> Oh the wold, the wold, the wold!

As John McEnroe might have said, the man cannot be serious. But he was. And in 1850!

But do we have to take sides in an 80-year-old argument? Can't we like Hardy's poem and cummings' too? Actually I do. I like some poems by TS Eliot, and other poems by Walter de la Mare. The argument between the old and the new is ageless. JS Bach was old-hat in his day and Shakespeare was criticised by Ben Jonson, who believed in 'High Art', for philistine populism – always a danger for poets who sell a lot of copies. John Ruskin, the Victorian critic, lashed the Old Guard when he was young and lashed the Young Turks (James McNeill Whistler) when he was old. I myself am inclined to grumble about those Young Turks – but I might be wrong. Tolstoy was wrong about Shakespeare and Ruskin was wrong about Whistler. WS Gilbert was wrong about Swinburne and Wilde.

Whatever you think, there is no doubt that Modernism happened and that it changed the artistic landscape. Why did it happen? The roots are deep and I think may be traced back to those Romantics a century before. Shelley, who seriously considered a career as a chemist and mixed up explosive potions in his rooms at Oxford, said that *poets* – not scientists – are the unacknowledged legislators of mankind. *Unacknowledged* legislators – the phrase has a frenzied, defensive air about it. Shelley knew he could never be an MP (who would nominate him, who elect him?), much less a Secretary of State like Milton. For the rich and powerful of his day Art was an amusement, a recreation; it had nothing to do with real life and they ignored it. Shelley tried appealing over their heads directly to the people, but the populace didn't trust him. As Marx remarked drily, when aristocrats set up as popular leaders, the people see coats of arms imprinted on their backsides and keep their heads down.

The first question to ask is the old Latin one: 'Cui bono?' Poetry? Who wants it? Who needs it? Who is *paying* for it? Poets in democracies have lost the aristocratic patrons they toadied to for funds and failed to find a mass audience to replace them. 'People', said the great utilitarian philosopher Jeremy Bentham, 'are free to choose pushpin [darts?] over poetry, and most of the time they do.' So who pays? Government committees and quangos that can be worse than the Lords and Ladies they replaced. Read the poet Roy Fuller's autobiography *Spanner and Pen* for the horrors of some Arts committees. But we poets should be polite – without Arts funding very few poetry presses would exist at all!

Poets who find they have no real audience (what Larkin calls 'paying customers') start talking among themselves in an exclusive language, like men talking about football to escape from their wives. An exclusive language about exclusion and superiority. Ezra Pound – energetic, witty and intelligent – started out as TS Eliot's mentor (Eliot called him, sincerely, *il miglior fabbro*, the better poet) and finished up broadcasting fascism for Mussolini. Does it have to happen like this? It is all rather depressing so, as the atheist said of Christianity, let us hope it is not true.

Actually it is not true, not wholly. Modern poetry is rarely incomprehensible. There is no poetic equivalent of the Turner Prize for 'mystification and outrage'. On the contrary, a typical fault of British poetry over the last half-century has been a rather clumsy pedestrianism, as the poet strives harder and harder for clarity, sincerity, unpretentiousness – to be a chap talking to chaps, or just one of the girls. Some have become *ludic*. Ludic?

What does 'ludic' mean?

None of my dictionaries thinks that the word exists at all – my PC gives me 'ludicrous' when I ask for it. But Professor David Crystal's excellent *Language Play* expounds 'The Ludic View of Language' in Chapter 1.

Rather than ludicrous, it's more helpful to think of ludo, because 'ludic' means 'game-playing' and ludic poetry is poetry that likes playing games – mostly language games. The word is new, the thing much older. In the 1840s Thomas Hood was irrepressibly ludic (resist the urge to let your eye skip to the end):

> No!
>
> No sun – no moon!
> No morn – no noon –
> No dawn – no dusk – no proper time of day –
> No sky – no earthly view –
> No distance looking blue –
> No road – no street – no 't'other side the way' –
> No end to any Row –
> No indications where the crescents go –
> No top to any steeple –
> No recognitions of familiar people –
> No courtesies for showing 'em –

No knowing 'em! –
No travelling at all – no locomotion,
No inkling of the way – no notion –
    'No go' – by land or ocean –
    No mail – no post –
No news from any foreign coast –
No Park – no Ring – no afternoon gentility –
    No company – no nobility –
No warmth, no cheerfulnes, no healthful ease,
    No comfortable feel in any member –
    No shade, no shine, no butterflies, no bees,
No fruits, no flowers, no leaves, no birds –
    November!

This is the 'Look no hands!' virtuousity that some poets seem to deprecate (*see* also Chapter 11 on rhyme). Not me, I love word games. Gavin Ewart wrote a one-word poem; Don Paterson wrote a no-word poem. Clever? Certainly. Why despise cleverness? Most, perhaps all, poetry involves elements of game-playing, and Postmodernism is particularly keen on games because it hates the whole idea of 'high' or 'serious' Art.

Postmodernism

'Postmodernism [that which comes after Modernism] is notoriously difficult to define,' says Christina Howells in the Encarta Encyclopedia. She goes on to describe 'junk Post-modernism' and the growing popularity of 'camp' and 'kitsch'. Professor Christopher Norris – cooler, more ironic (more Post-modernist, perhaps) – says in *The Oxford Companion to Philosophy*:

> Postmodernism is a term deployed in a variety of contexts … for things which seem to be related – if at all – by a laid-back pluralism of styles and a vague desire to have done with the pretensions of high modernist culture.

In fact, Postmodernism seems more easily defined by what it is *against* than what it is *for*. I might be Postmodernist; I certainly have more than a vague desire to have done with the 'pretensions of high modernist culture'. And the word ludic keeps cropping up: Postmodern Art is ludic; it plays games and hates 'seriousness'.

Good reasons for hating 'seriousness'

There is *la trahison des clercs* in the first part of the last century: the treason of the writers with bad politics – anti-democratic, racist politics – which most of us think were very bad indeed. Many Modernists such as Pound, Eliot and Yeats were involved in, or at least sympathetic to, fascism, anti-semitism ('the jew is underneath the lot' said Eliot) and hatred of the masses. Yeats died and Eliot put the lid on it as Hitler's power grew. Pound, alas, did not – although he repented in old age. If treasonous tosh is where high seriousness leads, then perhaps it is time for a few jokes.

But there is another reason for being suspicious of seriousness. Serious Art claims to want to make us better people. But better for what? Better for what our rulers have got lined up for us. Plato, a poet in his youth, threw the poets out of his Republic. Why? *Because they were not serious enough.* I am grateful to Les Murray in *The Paperbark Tree* for drawing my attention to these remarks of the poet Basil Bunting:

> Utilitarianism is the religion of the West in this century, as it was through most of the last century ... It is wrong to loaf and gawp about instead of working steadily at something useful, and of course it is wrong and foolish to write poetry unless it can be seen to purify the dialect of the tribe or keep the plebs in order or perform some other useful function.

We should all remember this secret agenda of our 'betters' and, like Robert Lowell who shunned President Kennedy's 'Camelot', *have nothing to do with it.* When I visit schools I know one of my functions is to help children pass exams and to assist with the literacy hour. I don't think that poetry is about exams, or even government ideas of literacy. What do I do? I take the money, read some poems – mine and other people's – then show the children how they can make their own, just as I hope to show you.

So what is Art for? Art is not *for* anything. 'All Art is quite useless', said Oscar Wilde; it is an end in itself, something we do because we want to do it, something we do because we are human. Why do I write? I write because I can. So let us play with words, remembering that all Art is play, as the German poet Schiller remarked somewhere.

Exercise 3: Ludic poetry

1. Write a piece whose first word begins with an 'a', second word with a 'b' and so on. You can cheat with 'x'. See how far down the alphabet you can get.

> Abraham brings Catherine diamond earrings from Glastonbury. Henrietta is jealous. Kenneth leaves Melissa nineteen opalescent pearls. Queenie (rather saintly!) takes Uncle Vlad's worthless, extravagantly yellow zircons.

2. Write a poem made up entirely of words of one syllable:

> We want ice cream
> Stop at the shop.
> Stop or we'll scream
> WE WANT ICE CREAM!

Not bad, but Phineas Fletcher in the 17th century could do much better.

> New light new love, new love new life hath bred;
> A light that lives by love, and loves by light;
> A love to him to whom all loves are wed;
> A light to whom the sun is dark as night.
> Eye's light, heart's love, the soul's sole life He is;
> Life, soul, Love, heart, light, eye and all are His;
> He eye, light, heart, love, soul; he all my joy and bliss.

I must confess that I have cheated a little and altered line 6 to keep to the rule. One of my favourite living poets, Wendy Cope, is very fond of one-syllable words: 'My heart has made its mind up', 'Pick up the phone before it is too late', 'The poets talk. They talk a lot'.

3. Somebody wrote a French novel without the letter 'e' and somebody else translated it into English, again without the letter 'e'. Perhaps a novel is going a bit far – here is an 'e'-less Nursery Rhyme

> Tiny Tim
> Has lost his goats.

Tim calls and calls.
Patrick! Joan! Palumbo!
I can't find you.

Don't worry, Tim.
Goats do OK.
Goats always know a way back.

Try a different one.

4. Write a poem allowing yourself only one vowel (I would not recommend 'u' unless you want to drive yourself mad). This is called a *univocalic* poem. Here's the start of an 'o' poem:

Down, down to London (or Oxford) Town
Dogs go bow-wow
Hogs root, motors toot,
Boots go, to, fro . . .

Ostrogoths . . . bottoms . . . bosoms . . . blossoms . . . orthodox monks . . .

5. Gavin Ewart claims to have invented the *daisychain* – each word begins with the last letter of the preceding word, as in this example by David Crystal: 'The escaping gangster ran next to old deserted docks'. Ewart's ingenious 'Daisychain for the Queen's Jubilee' can be found in *All My Little Ones*, perhaps the most irrepressibly ludic collection of poems ever written. This daisychain makes great use of the exclamation mark and cheats a little, but within the *spirit* of the thing, surely.

Youthful love! Everybody yearns so often. NEW whenever randiness strikes – such heaven! NEW wanton! NEW wisdom! Madness . . . sex exultingly, youthful love everlastingly!

A true daisychain will be circular, as this one is. You try. The problems are quite different from the problems of rhyme and scansion. Anyone who makes a daisychain that rhymes and scans see me at once!

Perhaps you don't call that stuff poetry. But poets do, and always have. The ancient Greeks wrote the first *concrete* poems – poems that make pictures, that have a strong visual element; Psalm 119, the very long one, is an acrostic – at least it is in Hebrew; Anglo-Saxons loved riddles.

Maybe it's still not *real* poetry. Such rules are of course arbitrary, and the results might be more ingenious than poetic. But poetry is best approached sideways, and perhaps, as you are striving to solve some verbal conundrum, the Muse may surprise you. The Irish poet, Austin Clarke, said his method of composition was to load himself with chains and then struggle free. Auden claimed that attention to formal matters saved poets from naked egotism, and it is certainly true that the free verse poets from Walt Whitman and DH Lawrence on do tend to talk a lot, and loudly, about themselves.

A ludic poet plays, plays with words. Which brings us neatly to the next chapter.

4. Words, Words, Words

A skeleton is made of bones,
A wall (perhaps) is made of stones,
A cottage cheese is made of curds
And a poem (look!) is made of ...

Words, not ideas, are a poet's trade. PJ Kavanagh, erstwhile poetry editor of *The Spectator*, was once introduced to schoolchildren as 'a poet – someone who *thinks* in a quite different way from ordinary people'. Kavanagh swears they looked at him oddly for the rest of the day.

This nonsense – that poets are benignly crazy – springs ultimately from our modern distinction between Art and Craft. Art is ideas for Ladies and Gents; Craft is handwork for artisans. The Classical world did not make this mistake. Latin *ars* is just a translation of Greek *techne* and both words are used of Art and Craft indiscriminately. Nowadays the Arts are considered far superior to mere Engineering, or they are until your car breaks down. I suggest you think of poems as little word machines and leave High Art to journalists.

Word games are the poet's gymnastics. Auden did the *Times* crossword every morning. That is beyond me, but I do try crosswords in trains.

That great charmer
Had teeth
I lead sir
Wild agitator means well
Brainy lot

Toilets
Stun aged hun – why?
Pink hair pill
I note word man
We all make his praise

Not a surreal poem but five anagrammatised politicians followed by five anagrammatised poets (answers at the end of the chapter). What have anagrams to do with poetry? Auden used one – a nubile tram – in his poem 'T the Great', and Kit Wright's 'Ecclesiastical History' is entirely made up of anagrams of *Poetry Review*.

Exercise 4: More ludic experiments

1. Four-letter words
Think of as many words of four letters as you can in just two minutes. Now write a piece of verse or prose made up entirely of four-letter words.

> What says that bird upon your gate?
> Alas! Alas! Bend down your grey head ...

2. Alphabetical qualities
The Spanish poet Miguel Cervantes went right through the alphabet, listing the qualities of the perfect lover. Of course, it doesn't have to be the *perfect* lover:

> Asinine, blethering, curmudgeonly, dense, empty-headed, futile, griping, hypocritical, intractable, juvenile, know-all, loafing, meddling, nit-picking, odious, puerile, querulous, stupid, tetchy, uninspiring, vulgar, whining, xenophobic, yobbish, zero-rated

3. Finders keepers

> Keep it dark.
>
> Keep your mouth shut and keep it dark.
> Keep your eyes skinned and keep it dark.
> Keep your head still and keep it dark.
> Keep your heart free and keep it dark.
> Keep your hair on and keep it dark.
> Keep your shirt on and keep it dark.
> Keep your hair shirt on and keep it dark.
> Keep your fingers crossed and keep it dark.
> Keep your mind on the job and keep it dark.
> Keep your ear to the ground and keep it dark.
> Keep your shoulder to the wheel and keep it dark.
> Keep your hands to yourself and keep it dark.

Keep your thoughts to yourself and keep it dark.
Keep your self to yourself and keep it dark.

Keep it dark.

Keep the ball rolling and keep it dark.
Keep the pot boiling and keep it dark.
Keep in step and keep it dark.
Keep in touch and keep it dark.
Keep a sharp look-out and keep it dark.
Keep a civil tongue in your head and keep it dark.
Keep taking the tablets and keep it dark.
Keep up with the Joneses and keep it dark.
Keep it dark.

Keep down the panic and keep it dark.
Keep time with the beat and keep it dark.
Keep track of the time and keep it dark.
Keep pace with the change and keep it dark.
Keep change for the phone and keep it dark.
Keep it dark.

Keep the wolf from the door and keep it dark.
Keep the wolf from your throat and keep it dark.
Keep the wolf from the dark and keep it dark.
Keep it dark.

Keep the dark from the dark and keep it dark.
Keep it dark.

Keep it spotless and keep it dark.

Take another verb from this list: bring, come, do, get, go, look, make, put, run, see, take, turn. Make a poem in a similar way. Similar, not the same.

Poems are not made out of ideas; they are made out of words – the truest saying about poetry and the most useful to know. Many bad poems have come about because the writer did *not* know it.

Great thoughts

A poet does not need great thoughts. Some of us have very silly ideas: Yeats believed in ectoplasm, MacDiarmid in Stalinism. I suppose it is because poetry is made up of words, and ideas are usually expressed in words, that we imagine that great poetry and great intellect are somehow connected.

Dante's Christian conception of God, says TS Eliot, is superior to Shakespeare's 'As flies to wanton boys are we to the Gods;/They kill us for their sport'. But if Dante's *philosophy* is better, it does not follow that his *poetry* is better. Of course we do not actually know Shakespeare's own thoughts about God; we only know those of his characters. When Keats spoke of Shakespeare's 'negative capability', he was referring to something many people have felt: that it is difficult to say what Shakespeare's opinion was about anything much and that it doesn't matter anyway. You could say Shakespeare doesn't count, because he is a dramatic poet. But isn't a lot of poetry, most poetry, a dramatisation of a state of mind?

> But at my back I always hear
> Time's winged chariot hurrying near
> And yonder all before us lie
> Deserts of vast Eternity.
> Thy beauty shall no more be found;
> Nor, in thy marble vault shall sound
> My echoing song; then worms shall try
> Thy long-preserved virginity:
> And your quaint honour turned to dust,
> And into ashes all my lust.
> The grave's a fine and private place,
> But none, I think, do there embrace.

Plenty of men have tried that argument before and after Marvell, and as an argument it stinks. One of my favourite poets is Omar Khayyam/Edward Fitzgerald.

> Come, fill the Cup, and in the fire of Spring
> The Winter garment of Repentance fling:
> The Bird of Time has but a little way
> To fly – and Lo! The bird is on the Wing.

What is he saying? That life is uncertain, so the best thing is to have lots of drink and sex. Thumbing through *The Faber Book of Murder* I find poems that celebrate killing husbands, wives, acquaintances, strangers – and animals! John Davidson's 'A Runnable Stag':

When the pods went pop on the broom, green broom,
And apples began to be golden-skinn'd
We harboured a stag in the Priory coomb
And we feather'd his trail up-wind, up-wind,
We feather'd his trail up-wind –
A stag of warrant, a stag, a stag,
A runnable stag, a kingly crop,
Brow, bay and tray and three on top,
A stag, a runnable stag,

I love that – but I don't want to hunt stags.

Shelley's Sonnet 'England in 1819' (you will find it in Chapter 13) is certainly political, but we read it *now* for the power of the invective, no longer caring much what he was inveighing against. Am I saying that poetry is just playing with words? No, it's more than that – but certainly it *is* playing with words. Emotion needs to be recollected, as Wordsworth said, in tranquillity; good writing is rarely dashed off in the white heat of passion. Recollected and then expressed in words – the best words in the best order, as Coleridge put it.

Old words and new words

The *Oxford English Dictionary* contains nearly 250,000 words; even the *Shorter Oxford* has 160,000. Professor David Crystal, in his invaluable *Cambridge Encyclopaedia of the English Language*, reckons that the average person knows – or recognises – around 40,000 words and could use about three-quarters of these. A well-read person's totals would be around 75,000 and 60,000 respectively. How many do you know?

I tried a simplified version of an experiment suggested by Professor Crystal. I looked at random at four pages of my *Shorter Oxford* and marked the words I knew (my passive vocabulary) and the words I might conceivably use (my active vocabulary). I then expressed them as a percentage of the total number of words in the sample. The results were gratifying, probably because I cheated: would I really use the word 'religionise', or recognise the word 'algazel'? Nevertheless there were many, many words I could not suppose, by the furthest stretch of my imagination, that I knew, had ever known or even seen (alexipharmic, gharry, uliginous). Perhaps I should increase my word-power *Readers'*

Digest-wise. Many poets are inveterate trawlers of dictionaries. Samuel Johnson even wrote one single-handed. (When told that the same task in France had required the combined efforts of 40 Frenchmen he was not at all surprised.) Hopkins used the old word 'sillion' (furrow) in 'The Windhover' (*see* also Chapter 13). Graves used 'vespertilian', meaning bat-like, to describe the devil's wings, perhaps because he liked the associations with evening and holy vespers. Larkin found, or allowed Monica Jones to find for him, the words 'losel' (a worthless person) and 'loblolly' (bumpkin) for the same line of verse. Poets are great renovators and renewers of the language.

The Dorset poet William Barnes wished to purify English of alien forms, by which he meant all French, Latin and Greek borrowings. He thought, by doing this, to make the language more easily understood by ordinary people. Purifying would suggest a cutting-down, but of course Barnes needed to invent as well. He came up with thousands of new words including 'birdlore', 'book-lore' and 'starlore' (all of which I rather like) for the Latinate ornithology, literature and astronomy. I think my favourite Barnes-word is 'folkdom'; it means democracy. What do you suppose 'hearsomeness' and 'forewit' are? And are you always 'soothfast'?

It may seem to you, as it does to me, that Barnes' project was hopeless from the start; as far as I know none of his words has passed into the language. Anyway, this 'purifying' is probably not a good idea. Apart from its unfortunate associations, which are not Barnes' fault, all such projects are probably doomed to failure – take George Bernard Shaw's spelling and punctuation reform, for example, or the various attempts to purge our language of Americanisms, vulgarisms and so on.

A writer *can* introduce new words – neologisms – to the language, though whether they will stay there is anybody's guess. Dylan Thomas had a way with words. I find 'brawned womb' and 'dogdayed pulse' on the first page of his collected poems, and though 'brawned' is in the dictionary, 'dogday' as a verb certainly is not. 'Kissproof' is not in my dictionary either; though it is well known now in association with lipsticks; perhaps Thomas was the first to use it, or one of the first. Roger McGough invents a pleasant verb when he says 'we ... arminarmed across the lawn', and a flick through my selected EE Cummings gives me 'outglory' (verb) and 'whying' (asking why).

These are not so much inventions as extensions, and of course that is how language grows. Words conjured out of nothing are rare. If they did not look like other words, how would you ever know what they meant? Wendy Cope has created the acronymic 'tump' (Totally Useless Male Poet): it certainly *sounds* good – all clumpy and mugwumpy. The poem that coined most new words must be Lewis Carroll's 'Jabberwocky':

'Twas brillig and the slithy toves
Did gyre and gimble in the wabe.
All mimsy were the borogroves
And the mome rath outgrabe.

Humpty-Dumpty goes on to tell Alice what it means:

'That's enough to begin with,' Humpty Dumpty interrupted: 'there are plenty of hard words there. 'Brillig' means four o'clock in the afternoon – the time when you begin broiling things for dinner.'

'That'll do very well,' said Alice: 'and 'slithy'?'

'Well, 'slithy' means 'lithe and slimy'. 'Lithe' is the same as 'active'. You see it's like a portmanteau – there are two meanings packed up into one word.'

Such words are not the prerogative of poets: *motel, brunch, smog, chunnel* and *guesstimate* are all 'portmanteaus' in Carroll's sense. Journalists (particularly headline-writers) and advertisers are making them up all the time, and most die an unlamented death. Edward Lear invented words too; his most famous coinage must be 'runcible', used of hats and spoons, but he doesn't explain what it means – you have to intuit it. Anthony Burgess, who began as a poet, invented a slang based on Russian for Alex in *A Clockwork Orange*:

He looked a malenky bit poogly when he viddied the four of us like tat, coming up so quiet and polite and smiling...

'Poogly' is good but I prefer Russell Hoban's *Riddley Walker*, about a 12-year-old boy who wanders through East Kent in a ruined future where towns have decayed into settlements such as Fork Stoan, Widders Bel and Horny Boy, and where he encounters the Wes Mincer, the Pry Mincer and the Ardship of Cambry. Hoban produces a convincing novelist's explanation for these formations (writing has practically died out, so words mutate into others that sound the same – malapropisms in fact), but that isn't why they appeal to me.

And Hardy, challenged over a word, burrowed through the OED before triumphantly finding his source – only to have his triumph soured when it was pointed out that the only authority quoted was Hardy himself.

Plus words and minus words

Roget's Thesaurus is a book no poet should be without. If we turn to a simple word in the index, let us say the word 'big', we find three others – 'great', 'large' and 'important', corresponding, perhaps, to three related but separable meanings: 'big' money, 'big' car and 'big' day. Under 'large' we find this, slightly shortened list:

> great, big, king-size, jumbo, massive, ample, monumental, whacking, whopping, elephantine, megalithic, immense, enormous, vast, mighty, grandiose, monstrous, colossal, gigantic, Brobdignagian, Titanic, Herculean, Gargantuan, outsize

Most of these words are 'plus' words; they describe desirable things or states of affairs. Bill Gates has a *big* salary. Of course he does. He has more than that: he has a *king-size, whacking, whopping, enormous, colossal, gigantic* salary (all plus words) and I wish I had one too. No I don't. His salary is so big I do not approve of it at all: the man has a *grandiose, monstrous, outsize* salary. These are 'minus' words

I have a healthy appetite and I like a big dinner. Some might say my figure was ample. On the other hand my neighbour is disgustingly *obese*. It's the *gargantuan* dinners he eats. No wonder he looks so *elephantine*. You may remember a word game that goes like this:

> I have input; you must nit-pick; he invariably moans.
> I am svelte and slender; you are skinny; she's a bag of bones.
>
> I'm romantic; you're a ladies' man: he's always on the job.
> I'm sophisticated; you're a bit class-conscious; she's a snob.
>
> Ours is antique classic; yours is second-user; theirs is junk.
> I'm amusing and vivacious; you're a chatterbox; she's drunk.

I'm curvaceous; you're full-figured; she's disgustingly obese.
We've been slandered; you're quite dodgy; they're all known to the
    police.

I've a theory; you've got views; he's just a gambler with a hunch.
I'm a poet; you're a dreamer; she's completely out to lunch.

Advertisers know all about plus words. A big brewing company
discovered through market research that 80% of beer was sold to
20% of the customers. In other words, they needed to appeal to
mountain-bellied sots (minus words). They could hardly say that,
so their agency came up with the slogan: 'Bulstrode's Beer [or
whatever it was] – great when you're *having more than one!*'

What has this to do with poetry? Let us look at Keats' 'The Eve
of Saint Agnes' again. The example was suggested, I think, by IA
Richards:

> Full on the casement shone the wintry moon
> And threw warm gules on Madeline's fair breast

A *casement* is, technically, a particular kind of window that opens
in a particular kind of a way, as opposed to a sash or a window
that opens by tilting. But Keats is not thinking of this. Casements
are, more importantly for him, romantic windows, 'magic
casements opening on faery lands forlorn' as he says elsewhere.
There have probably been too many casements in poetry since
Keats, and it has become a cliché – which is nothing more than an
overworked image. A *wintry* moon? Wintry is less of a plus word
than its counterpart *summery*. We have wintry smiles, which are
not reassuring, so a wintry moon is not only a moon in winter; it
carries a hint of threat with it, contrasting with the *warm* (warm
is a plus word, much more so than hot) gules on Madeline's
breast, another plus word. What is *gules*? My dictionary tells me
it is 'red as a heraldic colour'. Why didn't Keats just say red? Why
does he say in another stanza, 'the argent [another heraldic
colour] revelry'? We know perfectly well why, just as we know
that the word *fair* is nearly always a plus-word – 'fair hair, fair
skin, fair face'. White, on the other hand, though it *can* be positive
– 'white as snow' – is often less so – 'white as a sheet' – or very
negative indeed – 'white as death', Coleridge's 'white as leprosy'.

> ## *Exercise 5: The colour of colours*
> Take a colour and make a list of all the common usages you can think of.
>
> > green as grass, green about the gills, green fingers, a green thought in a green shade, the Green party, green with envy, eat your greens, green and pleasant land, giving the green light, not so green as he's cabbage-looking, eat your greens, green pastures, the green, green grass of home, mountain greenery, greenery-yallery, green field sites . . .
>
> I'm sure you could extend this list. Most of the uses of green are plus-uses, but not all of them. A similar list of black phrases would probably show a preponderance of minus-uses, don't you think? Yes, the language does have a built-in racism about it. And a built-in anti-feminism too: 'boyish' has many more positive connotations than 'girlish', doesn't it? What about 'mannish' and 'womanish' though? Both bad, both minus. The plus words are 'manly' and 'womanly', though I wonder if either of those – and particularly the second – are usable at all nowadays except in unserious contexts.
>
> Write a poem whose title contains the colour you have chosen.

Answers to anagrams (*see* pp. 26–7)
The politicians are, in order: Margaret Thatcher, Ted Heath, Disraeli, William Ewart Gladstone, Tony Blair. 'Elect me – I'm alien!' spells Michael Heseltine, which is nice. The poets are TS Eliot, Wystan Hugh Auden, Philip Larkin, Andrew Motion, William Shakespeare.

Barnes' resurrections (*see* p. 31)
I am sure you worked out that if you are forewitted, soothfast and hearsome, then you are prudent, truthful and obedient.

5. Poems About . . .

What are poems about? In one sense they are always about yourself, as the film director Fellini pointed out.

> Each man in his life writes the same book again and again because each man is imprisoned in his own life. But it doesn't matter.

If Art, if poetry, is always about yourself, doesn't that make it rather self-regarding? The poet Norman MacCaig says no:

> I write about things I have myself experienced or, less often, of things I have observed in other people. This is not so egotistical as it may seem for, since I am not in any way an eccentric man, I believe these experiences are shared and recognised by most other people.

Shouldn't poetry transcend the purely personal? EE Cummings tells us how his puritan New England education taught him that 'the one and only thing that mattered about a poem was what it said'.

> A good poem was a poem which did good, and a bad poem was a poem which didn't: Julia Warde Howe's Battle Hymn of the Republic was a good poem because it helped free the slaves. Armed with this ethical immutability, I composed canticles of comfort on behalf of the grief-stricken relatives of persons recently deceased; I implored healthy Christians to assist poor-whites afflicted with the Curse of the Worm (short for hookworm); and I exhorted right-minded patriots to abstain from dangerous fireworks on the 4th of July.

He needed, he said, to *un*learn this. So do we all. An earthquake, a war, the death of a princess or a child, will inspire sheaves of poems. Adults write them. Children up and down the land are sat down in classrooms to write them: I read in a newspaper an 11-year-old's prize-winning verse exhorting us to join the Euro. They turn up in their hundreds and thousands in poetry competitions, transparently sincere. But rarely, oh so rarely, any good.

A poem written or conceived as a poem with a *message* is too often not a poem at all. It wants to be prose; the poetic form is pasted on afterwards as a decorative effect. It is true that many poets – Ben Jonson, Pope, Browning, Tennyson, Yeats – have made use of prose drafts, but these seem usually to have been more like notes and the final poem often bears only a tangential relationship to them (*see* also Chapter 15). Don't versify a message. You are divorcing the form from the content and you shouldn't do that. Larkin said that the idea for a poem and a snatch of it came to him simultaneously – in other words that the form and content started indivisibly one.

Yet poets do write poems about given subjects. They do it for money. When I am commissioned I can expect £100–250, much more than the general market rate for a poem (£40 at the time of writing). Better-known poets get more, often much more. We have to live, however remote the necessity may seem to other people. A commissioned poem is called an 'occasional verse', not because it is written occasionally, but because it is in response to an occasion.

Occasional verse

The commissions that work best for me are those I might have written anyway, where the commission seems no more than a prompt. Sometimes it really does present itself as a scrap of verse or a rhythm. I was asked by the editor of *Poetry Review* to write a sonnet about two famous and influential critics, Al Alvarez and Ian Hamilton. Now these are rather slashing critics, by which I mean they have strong likes and dislikes which come out most powerfully as dislikes – ideas about how poetry should be written and particularly about how it should not be written. Alvarez, for instance, sees English post-war poetry as prissy, straight-laced and buttoned-up. Americans, by contrast, are big and bold and unpredictable and violent. Like a Clint Eastwood Western, it struck me – I heard the thunder of hooves and a scrap of the poem was there:

> Oh the critics are coming! Their hoofbeats are drumming.
> There's blood on their saddles, they shoot for the heart.

Once I had found the image of critics as deadeye Wyatt Earps, and the galloping metre (**dah**dede **dah**dede) – a memory of Browning ('How They Brought The Good News from Ghent to Aix') and Scott ('Young Lochinvar'), both of which I learned at school:

> I **sprang** to the **saddle** and **Boris** and **he**,
> I **gall**oped, Dirk **gall**oped, we **gall**oped all **three** ...

and

> There **ne'er** was a **knight** like the **young** Lochinvar!

once I had got this, the poem practically wrote itself. As Jorge Luis Borges, the Argentinian poet, says, it is much easier to write in a strict metrical form because half the work is already done for you.

Does this sound soulless and mechanical? How can you 'look into your heart and write' (Sir Philip Sidney) to a prescribed pattern? Very easily. John Dryden, king of the occasional verse, claimed a rhyme had often helped him to the sense. In other words he was not sure what he was going to say before he wrote down a list of possible rhymes in response to an initial line. This is puzzling to people who think he should have had the naked inspiration first, then clothed it with poetry. But can a thought exist independently of the words used to express it? Marx's proposition:

> Man is born free but everywhere he is in chains.

could be paraphrased. Any paraphrase will oppose the natural, right state of humanity (freedom!) to the way things are (slavery!). But if you lose the image of a prisoner in chains, you lose a great deal. You lose the pressing sense of injustice and the sense that such chains can and will be broken if the prisoner just has the strength and the courage. A paraphrase is an abstraction – consequently not the *thought* at all, but some anaemic, watered-down version.

I feel about Yeats' Spiritualism rather as I feel about the cardboard fairies at the bottom of the garden that deceived Sir Arthur Conan Doyle. I am fairly unmoved by the clangorous name-dropping of ancient sages (Pythagoras, Plotinus) and all the machinery of 'perning' in 'gyres' and it is a very moot point whether Yeats belived it all himself. There is more than the whiff of fakery here. Yet 'Sailing to Byzantium' and 'Byzantium', for

38

instance, are among his greatest poems, among the greatest poems of the 20th century. Why? Read them and see. Read them and see the simple, the beautiful, yes the magical arrangement of simple words on a page which makes them 'poetic touchstones' as Matthew Arnold calls them. The poems are not fakes, though Yeats himself – sometimes and in some moods – may have been.

What about sincerity?

Oscar Wilde said:

> A little sincerity is a dangerous thing and a great deal of it is absolutely fatal.

I go into schools to read poems and show the children how to write them. I say that writing poems is different from writing essays because you don't want to plan a poem too carefully beforehand. Poems whisper behind their hands and you must listen attentively; you can't order them about. A Muse directs you, and not the other way about. Remember those essay subjects you were given in school – The Commonwealth or The Nuclear Holocaust (nowadays it might be The European Experience or Global Warming). You stare at an empty page. What *do* you think about these important issues?

A touch of autobiography

I was once supposed to write a weighty editorial for our school magazine about the death of President Kennedy. I tried, and failed ignominiously, a failure that niggled for years until I read Johnson's coat-trailing remark that 'public affairs vex no man'. Boswell expostulated that the Whigs – Johnson was a staunch Tory – certainly *did* vex him, but Johnson was having none of it: 'Sir, I have never slept an hour less, nor eaten an ounce less meat. I would have knocked the factious dogs on the head, to be sure, but I was not *vexed*.'

Why are Laureate poems generally so bad? Betjeman, Hughes and Motion have all written well, but not, I think, as Laureates. Royalty and the Millennium do not engage them poetically and they have to fake it. We all do sometimes. I commiserate with my daughter over the England football team's latest abject performance, not because I care about football but because I care about her. I don't say it doesn't matter because it obviously does – to her, now. But I wouldn't write a poem about it.

That's all very well, but what about important things? Let's talk about important things. The death that mattered to me when I was young was not an American President's but my mother's. Have I written a poem about it? I have written three. The first stole up on me. I was looking, with my children, at an old photograph of Mum sitting in the garden with my brother, my sister and me. She was wearing a straw hat and squinting into the sun – a happy photograph, a happy and secure childhood until ... That 'until' led me into the poem – 30 years later. The others were almost occasional. I wrote a book-long sequence about my childhood which had ended (it seemed to me) with my mother's death. I needed a poem of 20 lines with a particular rhyme scheme. I put it off and put it off, then wrote two, quite quickly, and used them both. I now think that the second was the real poem and am in the process of turning the first – about bargaining with God for my mother's life – into a short story which is what it always wanted to be.

Would I have written those poems without the necessity, without the printer at the door? Good poems *are* written to order. Betjeman wrote one of his best for a magazine competition; Auden wrote 'Night Mail' for a documentary film. My favourite occasional poem is Marvell's 'An Horatian Ode upon Cromwell's Return from Ireland':

> He nothing common did or mean
> Upon that memorable Scene;
> But with his keener eye
> The axe's edge did try:
> Nor called the Gods, with vulgar spite
> To vindicate his helpless Right,
> But bowed his comely Head
> Down as upon a Bed.

But it is more difficult to write good poems about concentration camps or assassinations than about your child in the supermarket, perhaps because abstractions tend to creep in. Poetry works best where those 'big words fail to fit' as the poet Derek Enright has it. Kit Wright's 'George Herbert's Other Self in Africa' is certainly about mass starvation, guilt, powerlessness and anger.

Wright confronts these big words indirectly through a literary exercise (*see* below). Here is part of Herbert's 'The Collar'. He was a 17th parson who turned away from 'the world' and sometimes, like Hopkins 200 years later, regretted it:

> I struck the board, and cried, No more.
> I will abroad.
> What? Shall I ever sigh and pine?
> My lines and life are free; free as the road,
> Loose as the wind, as large as store.
> Shall I be still in suit?
> Have I no harvest but a thorn
> To let me blood, and not restore
> What I have lost with cordial fruit?

And now Wright's poem:

> Thinking another way
> To tilt the prism,
> I vowed to turn to light
> My tenebrism
> And serve not light
> But day.
>
> Surely, I cried, the sieves
> Of love shake slow
> But even. Love subsists
> Though pressed most low:
> As it exists
> Forgives.
>
> But my stern godlessness
> Rose through the sun,
> Admonished me: Fat heart,
> So starving's fun?
> Whom have they art
> To bless?
>
> Thereat my false thought froze,
> Seeing how plain
> The field was where they died,
> How sealed their pain,
> And I replied,
> God knows.

Exercise 6: About what?

This exercise is designed to stop you writing head-on *about* things. It will work if you don't think too consciously about it but let the words take you where they want to go. Then perhaps you may ambush a poem.

Take a line of verse – something well known and, if possible, something you like, or at least something you have a relation-ship with. This one, perhaps:

> I should have been a pair of ragged claws.

Write a poem which contains these nine words. No, that's too easy. Write a poem of nine lines which contains these nine words at the rate of one per line. Still too easy: the words are very ordinary words – perhaps it would be different if the line were 'The multitudinous seas incarnadine', though in that case the poem would be only four lines long and perhaps we should want to take the next line as well. Use the words in the proper order. Begin the poem with 'I' and end it with 'claws'. Set yourself a time limit – 15 minutes or maybe 20.

Here is a poem of mine. It uses a different line (actually two lines):

Sleep

We picnic in the park after the show;
There **are** several other families doing the same –
It *is* **such** a very English summer evening.
'What's all this **stuff**?' says my daughter, probing the pate de foie
Suspiciously before rejecting it. **As** if we had stumbled
Into another of those costume-dramas (**dreams** and nightmares
Exquisitely dressed, sensitively lit), her blue eyes **are** wide and oh
She's beautiful, breakable, one of those shepherdesses **made** of porcelain.
'Goose-livers? *Goose-livers*! Aw Jeeze, Dad, you're having me **on**!'

And what do they mean, these moments in time
When **our** apprehensions seem suddenly heightened
For a **little** space (it's never more than that), when

We see our **lives** perfected, as if they belonged
To someone else entirely. **Are** we deceived? Probably. What's to
    come
Is far from unsure – the **curtained**-off bed, everything slowing
    down,
Names, faces forgotten. Aw Jeeze, Dad, **with** new drugs,
Micro-surgery, what-not, it's a thousand guineas to **a** bloody
    euro,
There's *years* yet before the big one, the big, you know.

This is free verse with a pattern, though without the high-lighting it might remain a private pattern. Dylan Thomas wrote a poem of 100 lines where the first line rhymed with the last, the second with the second last and so on. Of course no reader would be aware of this unless it was pointed out, but does that matter if the structure allowed Thomas to write a good poem?

We need some other way of structuring poems apart from the tyranny of a subject. It doesn't have to be rhyme or metre, but we need *something*. Much modern poetry is born from the search for these new structures. Poets who repeat effects too often write stale stuff. How did Shakespeare write over 150 sonnets, then? One answer is that he did not, in general, repeat his effects; that the form of the sonnet allows a great deal of variation. Another answer is that some sonnets *are* stale, perfunctory, etc. – though remarkably few, and rarely all the way through. Gavin Ewart tried to write each new poem in a different form to keep him sharp.

Not all your poems will work; some will be failures. Make them fresh failures rather than old, tired failures. Keep experimenting, trying – in the felicitous words of Keats and Pound, to 'keep your English up' and 'make it new'.

This is a chapter about words. Words are a poet's tools. They are the best tools, the only tools we have for poetry, but they are not to be trusted too far. Here is what Ted Hughes says about them (you will find it in 'Poetry in the Making' in his book *Winter Pollen*):

Words are tools, learned late and laboriously and easily forgotten, with which we try to give some part of our experience a more or less permanent shape inside ourselves. They are unnatural, in a way, and far from being ideal for their job. For one thing, a word has its own definite meanings. A word is its own little solar system of meanings. Yet we want it to carry some part of our meaning, of the meaning of our experience.

Yet you must write about *something*? Then choose yourself, as I said initially – not in a boastful, self-aggrandising way, but simply as an example. Touch others' hearts by showing your own. Recline into your own life. Both these pieces of good advice are from Hardy.

A writer's life is often uneventful. Emily Dickinson's was so uneventful that for most of it she never left the house. Larkin, asked by Kingsley Amis whether he had any secret hopes of a Nobel Prize, answered, sardonically, typically:

> I thought they might be keeping it warm for a chap like me – you know, a chap who never *writes* anything or *does* anything or *says* anything.

But the man who didn't *do* anything or *say* anything (or even *write* so very much) nevertheless found inspiration in his own sedentary, single life. And though he failed to win the Nobel – it wasn't England's turn – he won many other prizes.

6. Metaphors, similes and images

Living language is very pictorial. When cricket commentator and poet John Arlott said that the Australian batsman Ken Mackay was 'a man shaped like a bottle', he gave us a picture of squatness, sturdiness, rotundity, breadth of shoulder and perhaps a lack of grace. He gave us an *image* of Mackay. Images can be *similes*, as here (Mackay is *like* a bottle), or *metaphors*.

Metaphor, says my *OED*, is the figure of speech in which a name or descriptive term is transferred to some object *to which it is not properly applicable* (my italics):

> Let Sporus tremble – 'What? that Thing of silk?
> Sporus, that mere white Curd of Ass's milk?
> Satire or Sense alas! can Sporus feel?
> Who breaks a Butterfly upon a Wheel?'
> Yet let me flap this Bug with gilded wings,
> This painted Child of Dirt that stinks and sings,
> Whose buzz the Witty and the Fair annoys,
> Yet Wit ne'er tastes, and Beauty ne'er enjoys,
> So well-bred Spaniels civilly delight
> In mumbling of the Game they dare not bite.

Sporus is not really a thing, a white curd or a butterfly – Alexander Pope just says that he is (he also says he is *like* a spaniel). Some claim you can't have poetry without metaphor, that the use of metaphorical language is the only sure sign that poetry is going on. But when Othello says of Desdemona:

> She loved me for the dangers I had passed
> And I loved her that she did pity them,

when the Ancient Mariner says of the heat and the drought in a great calm:

> Water, water everywhere
> And all the boards did shrink;
> Water, water, everywhere,
> Nor any drop to drink,

when the anonymous, homesick sailor bursts out:

> Christ, that my love were in my arms
> And I in my bed again!

I do not see any metaphors, but if this is not poetry I'll eat my poet's hat. Of course the sailor personifies the wind in the first two lines of the poem:

> Western wind when wilt thou blow
> That the small rain down can rain?

Of course there is a celebrated simile 'as idle as a painted ship upon a painted ocean' in the previous stanza of Coleridge's poem; and of course Othello is a dab-hand if not at metaphor, then at least at simile:

> . . . one whose hand,
> Like the base Indian, threw a pearl away
> Richer than all his tribe . . .

Truly, you can scarcely open your mouth without falling into metaphor. In fact, you cannot have human language at all without metaphor – we are all poets *from the cradle*, which is a metaphor, though a thoroughly dead one.

What is most important about language is not its clarity – though we should try to be as clear as the subject allows – but its *invention*. We do not have languageless thoughts and then clothe them with appropriate words. 'How do I know what I mean until I see what I say?', as EM Forster said.

Thomas Hobbes, the 17th century philosopher who characterised human life in its natural state as 'solitary, poor, nasty, brutish and short' – thus showing a command of rhetoric many poets would envy – nevertheless said that the ideal language would be purged of metaphor. 'The wise man', he said, 'uses words as counters'. He was wrong, you can't use words like that; they do not stand for things-in-the-world in that sort of straightforward one-to-one relationship as, in other moods, he very well knew. In the (metaphorical) words of John Donne:

> On a huge hill,
> Cragged and steep, Truth stands, and he that will
> Reach her, about and about must go;
> And what the hill's suddenness resists, win so.

But truth is not like that – out there to be fetched; truth is within and difficult to recognise. Plato banished poets because they told lies. But it would not be sufficient to banish poets; Plato would have to banish language altogether, or invent a Hobbesian one (like Orwell's Newspeak) in which it was impossible to tell lies. Lies are, of course, opinions contrary to those of the rulers – Plato and his cronies.

A notable feature of Orwellian Newspeak was its small vocabulary. Orwell's idea was that if a language does not have a word for something then it ceases to exist, at least in the minds of the speakers of that language – assuming, presumably, that they speak no other. But languages will not be policed. The French language is jealousy guarded by an Academy which throws out 'dangerous' new words (English usually) that are considered inimical to French culture. Fortunately, and characteristically, French people pay no attention and go on speaking of *le fast food*, *les sex shops*, *le foot(ball)*, *le pull(over)* just as if the Academy did not exist at all. When I learned Latin I discovered that what they were teaching me was not what the Romans actually *said*, but a literary construct made from 'correct' prose writers Caesar and Cicero and Livy, who tended to be, frankly, rather boring. Who taught me what the language, and therefore the Roman reality, was really like? Why poets, rememberers for the human race, scurrilous fellows like Catullus, Martial and Petronius.

One of my favourite new words (it is less than 100 years old) is the cricketing term 'googly'. It is used of a ball which, when bowled, does just the opposite of what the batsman expects and ends up not only getting him out, but making him look ridiculous as well. The *OED* says the word is 'of unknown origin', but it was obviously invented by a poet: a 'portmanteau' word (the term is Lewis Carroll's) made up of 'diddle' and 'goggle' and 'wobble' – and even 'ogle', perhaps, for the batsman sees the ball as enticing and attempts, fatally, to hit it for six. And before leaving cricket (I promise, I promise), can I mention the sometime player and cricketing journalist RC Robertson-Glasgow, nicknamed Crusoe because a Yorkshireman called Emmot Robinson complained he had been bowled 'by an old something-or-other I thought was dead called Robinson Crusoe'. Robinson's inspiration stuck, fitting Robertson-Glasgow's slightly raffish, googly-bowling image. Poetry belongs to everyone.

Exercise 7: *What's in a name?*

One way in which novelists allow the poetic side of their natures to escape is in the invention of names for their characters. These can be straight jokes, as when Trollope calls a doctor Fillgrave or Fielding calls a schoolmaster Thwackum. But it becomes poetry when Dickens calls his schoolmaster Squeers (squint + squash + queer + bleary + a lot of other words hovering on the fringes of your consciousness), or PG Wodehouse calls his unflappable gentleman's gentleman Jeeves (perhaps James – butlers and such were frequently called James – + sleek + sleeves). Bertie Wooster is a pretty good name too, particularly with the double-o in the middle. Bertie has two aunts, Aunt Agatha and Aunt Dahlia, one nice and one nasty. Which is which? If you didn't know, then you could surely guess. You don't have to write a novel, just think up suitable names for characters in the novel you *might* write. You can do this with someone else. Each of you write down the names of (say) three invented characters, exchange, and then decide what kind of a person each one is. Then compare that with what the original inventor of the name thought. To make the exercise fruitful you must avoid the Thwackum sort of name and go for the Squeers kind instead. It strikes me that Frank Richards' Quelch (squelch, quash) and Prout (shout, pry) are good schoolmasterly names too – he got Prout from Kipling's *Stalky & Co*. What do you think? Here is part of a classic 1920s detective story:

> A rumour round the village – something horrid
> At Foreskin Hall. It's 1933.
> The bishop's lying in the library,
> A boomerang embedded in his forehead.
> Superintendent Grouting, fat and florid,

> Reluctantly calls in the CID.
> They're baffled too. A classic mystery –
> Murder most foul and Passion very torrid.
> The Rural Dean discovered *in flagrante*
> With Lord 'Boy' Foreskin, Nanny peddling dope,
> A Blackshirt rally Friday at the vicar's,
> Bunty Persimmons prostrate in her knickers
> Before an image of the Anti-Pope.
> Nothing escapes the sleuthing dilettante.

Metaphor and simile

So when you say a thing is like another thing, then that is a simile.

1. My love is like a red, red rose
2. A diamond as big as the Ritz

When you say a thing *is* another thing – which it obviously is not – then that is a metaphor. In Andrew Marvell's 'To His Coy Mistress', 'vegetable love' is a metaphor: he wants to say that, given all the time in the world, his love would increase for ever.

> My vegetable love would grow
> Vaster than Empires and more slow

Any simile will become a metaphor if you suppress the 'like', and vice-versa.

The *epic simile* is borrowed from Homer. It is curious in being very long and involved, so long that you become more interested in the material of the simile than in its aptness. Here is an example from 'Paradise Lost'. Milton says Satan's spear is as tall as a ship's mast, but he doesn't leave it at that:

> His spear, to equal which the tallest Pine
> Hewn on Norwegian hills, to be the mast
> Of some great Admiral, were but a wand,
> He walked with ...

Before we return to Satan in Hell we have been to Norway and back. We have also moved forwards in time to Milton's own age, when ships were as big as the one he describes, and back again to

4004 BC (the supposed date of the Creation) when there weren't any ships at all. So the story of Adam and Eve encompasses the whole world and the whole history of the world – which of course it does, according to Milton.

Metaphor and ordinary language

Ordinary language is full of metaphor, as in this exchange overheard on a bus.

> Miss Price pinched my mobile, the old bat.
> Life's a pig, isn't it?

Miss Price is only metaphorically a bat. Life is only metaphorically a pig. And pinched is a metaphor too. Let us consider pigs.

> Pig out!
> Life's a pig.
> Stop pigging it in bed, your room's a pigsty
> The pigs arrested him
> Piggy eyes
> Piggy wives
> Take that, you swine!

Poor pigs – nasty little eyes, fat bottoms, horrible eating habits, sleeping all day – pure piggism.

> Wise as a pig, sleek as a pig,
> Cuddly and faithful and fair as a pig

No, I don't think it will catch on – though there are some nice literary pigs; I am thinking of the three little ones and Babe the sheep-pig. But metaphorical pigs in ordinary language have a very negative image. Lions, on the other hand, do pretty well – a lion heart and a leonine head are good things to have.

However, these ordinary-language metaphors are not the metaphors a poet particularly deals in. Poets are making it new, if you remember, and their metaphors should bring you up short. Marvell's love as a prize-winning marrow is certainly an unexpected image; it might even incline you to giggle. Poetry often treads the fine line between magnificence and falling flat on its face. Somewhere in Africa, likening a warrior to a hippopotamus is high praise, but you couldn't make that work here where hippos are comic creatures.

My love is like a 1. red, red rose
   2. white, white rose
   3. lily
   4. chrysanthemum
   5. dandelion
   6. daisy

I think most of us would agree that our loves could easily be 1, 2, 3 and just possibly 6, but not 4 or 5. It is difficult to be sure *why* my love could not be a chrysanthemum – some might think a chrysanthemum more beautiful than a rose, although I don't. Perhaps they have too many associations with garden centres and packets of seeds – there is not enough wildness about them. Dandelions are wild, but they are weeds, popping up scruffily all over the place. Obviously your love can't be like that, though she or he might conceivably be a daisy. But being like a daisy (fresh, perky, etc.) is a very different thing from being like a rose and the poem would be a very different kind of a poem.

Dead metaphors no longer have any force. For instance, the word 'explain' originally meant 'to lay out flat' and thus was used metaphorically when you spoke of explaining something to somebody. But it is a metaphor no longer. Nor, I think is the word 'poured' in an expression like 'the crowd poured from the football ground'. We ought to think – like water from a jug, but we don't. There is nothing wrong with a dead metaphor; we could hardly open our mouths without using some. What is worse is the *moribund metaphor*, beloved of politicians:

> Do you know where I'm coming from, know where I'm at?
> When they're moving the goalposts I keep a straight bat.
> In a game of two halves I keep serving straight aces
> To get a result on a regular basis,

This verse also contains some fine *mixed metaphors*. Metaphors make pictures; if two or more metaphors together make a picture which is ludicrous, then we say the metaphors are 'mixed'. Does Hamlet use a mixed metaphor when he speaks of taking up arms against a sea of troubles? I say no – the image of fighting against the sea is more noble than ludicrous. But Shakespeare gives Mark Anthony a ludicrous metaphor when he says:

> My heart is in the coffin there with Caesar,
> And I must pause till it come back to me.

His heart has been transformed into a pet, getting into coffins but always coming back in the end. Anthony is insincere, manipulative and politically devious; so he uses second-hand language, though the Roman plebeian crowd is too stupid to see it (Shakespeare had no great opinion of plebeian crowds).

Then there is the *second-hand metaphor*. A sea of troubles and a sea-change are fine images, but they are Shakespeare's and we should leave them to him. The man who first drove a coach-and-horses through an Act of Parliament may have startled his hearers to good effect, but we can't go on doing it. Why not? Because the words no longer conjure up the image. A sea-change is what happens to a corpse under water, but the politician doesn't mean that; he just means a big change. And nobody drives a coach-and-horses now.

So, studding your writing with metaphors will not transmute it into poetry. Sometimes the very plainest speech is what you want. In the ballad 'The Twa Corbies', a pair of corbies (crows) are discussing the 'new slain knight' who is their prospective lunch:

> As I was walking all alane,
> I heard twa corbies making a mane;
> The tane unto the t'other say,
> 'Where sall we gang and dine today?'

> 'In behint yon auld fail dyke,   [turf wall]
> I wot there lies a new slain knight;
> And naebody kens that he lies there,
> But his hawk, his hound and his lady fair,

> 'His hound is to the hunting gane,
> His hawk to fetch the wild-fowl hame,
> His lady's ta'en another mate,
> So we may mak our dinner sweet.

> 'Ye'll sit on his white hause-bane,   [neck-bone]
> And I'll pike out his bonny blue een;
> Wi ae lock o his gowden hair
> We'll theek our nest when it grows bare,   [thatch]

> 'Mony a one for him makes mane,
> But none sall ken where he is gane;
> O'er his white banes, when they are bare,
> The wind sall blaw for evermair.'

No metaphors there. But talking crows are obviously related to metaphor – real crows don't talk. The crows are symbols.

Symbols

A symbol is a symbol *of* something. The swastika is a symbol of the Nazi party; reversed, it is an Eastern symbol of good luck. The same symbol can stand for many things – it all depends on the context. What are the crows in the ballad symbolic of? Death, decay and evil and ill omens – yes, all of these. Crows are proverbially wise and long-lived; could that be relevant? I think so! But had the birds been doves or sparrows then we would have expected quite a different conversation to ensue.

> When I behold, upon the night's starred face
> Huge, cloudy symbols of a high romance
> And think that I may never live to trace
> Their shadows with the magic hand of chance . . .

The symbols Keats wants to trace are huge but cloudy; shadows traced anyway by magic and chance. If we are looking for a one-to-one equivalence for poetic symbols, we will not find it.

> Oh rose thou art sick!
> The invisible worm
> That flies in the night
> In the howling storm;
>
> Has found out thy bed
> Of crimson joy;
> And his dark secret love
> Does thy life destroy.

Is the worm Satan? Or a penis? In Blake's illustration it looks very like a worm. Actually it is all these things at once. Poetic symbols work *because* there is no one-to-one correspondence; they are multi-faceted and open our minds out to possibility.

Metaphors can be flashy and strained. Strained metaphors are a sure sign that the poet is operating on auto-pilot (and that in itself is a pretty tired metaphor, come to think of it). When the young John Dryden described the smallpox that killed Lord Hastings, he was surely thinking more of his own cleverness:

> Each little pimple had a tear in it
> To wail the fault its rising did commit...

And his contemporary, Richard Crashaw likened the eyes of a grief-stricken woman to:

> Two walking baths, two weeping motions,
> Portable and compendious oceans.

Could I find something similar in a modern poet's work? I could.

> Wind your wildering hair with sorrow
> Wind it with the night

As Kingsley Amis might have said – wind your *what* hair with *what*? And with *what*? Who wrote this stuff? Alas, I did.

A metaphor is bad when it is stuck onto the poem like those gold and silver glitter hearts my daughters used to stick onto their possessions and their persons. A metaphor is good when it is a part of what is being said, when it *is* what is being said.

> Tomorrow, and tomorrow and tomorrow
> Creeps in this petty pace from day to day
> To the last syllable of recorded time,
> And all our yesterdays have lighted fools
> The way to dusty death. Out, out brief candle!
> Life's but a walking shadow, a poor player
> That struts and frets his hour upon the stage
> And then is heard no more. It is a tale
> Told by an idiot, full of sound and fury,
> Signifying nothing.

The thing about Shakespeare, as someone said, is that he's so full of quotations. Tomorrow *creeps in* and yesterday deceived fools by *lighting the way* (a good thing to do) but not saying where the way was going (to death). *Life's ... a poor player* (Macbeth, a man of action, would have had a poor opinion of actors, and poets too, come to that); it is a *tale told by an idiot* (Macbeth is not politically correct about mental illness, either). It is through the metaphors, the images, that we see Macbeth's soul and understand his bottomless despair. The images change fast, as fast as Macbeth's thought, but we do not think of them as mixed metaphors because the effect is not ludicrous. At least not to us. Samuel Johnson could not believe Macbeth really said 'the blanket of the dark' because a blanket was, to him, a ludicrously unpoetic thing. He emended it to 'blank height' and was surely wrong to do so.

Let us sum up. Language is not a labelling system. The world of things and the world of language exist alongside one another; sometimes it is poetry that can jump the gap. Language without poetry does not exist and all language-users are poets at least part of the time.

Exercise 8: The anaphoric poem

Anaphora – repetition of the same word or phrase – is another of those things you were taught at school; if you weren't listening or have forgotten, let me remind you. Here is a part of Whitman's very long poem 'Song of Myself' (a katy-did is a grasshopper):

> Where the humming bird shimmers, where the neck of the long-
> lived swan is curving and winding,
> Where the laughing gull scoots by the shore, where she laughs
> her near-human laugh,
> Where bee-hives range on a gray bench in the garden, half hid by
> the high weeds,
> Where band-necked partridges roost in a ring with their heads
> out,
> Where burial coaches enter the arch'd gates of a cemetery,
> Where winter wolves bark amid wastes of snow and icicled trees,
> Where the yellow-crowned heron comes to the edge of the marsh
> at night and feeds upon small crabs,
> Where the splash of swimmers and divers cools the warm noon,
> Where the katy-did works her chromatic reed on the walnut-tree
> over the wall ...

Characteristically, Whitman just goes gloriously on and on. Nicky Jackowska is sparer. Perhaps she composed more couplets, then selected the best.

Conservatory for Ladies of Pleasure

I keep my orange in a glass house,
the hot wet leaves breathing against its skin.

I keep my blue dress in the refrigerator,
Soon a constellation of silver needles on the sleeves.

I keep my first ring on a high shelf,
The wind poked a finger through it, a love draught.

I keep my handkerchief in a shallow grave,
The heavy earth holds its life steady.

I keep my shoes up under the eaves,
To borrow from the chemistry of roofs.

I keep myself in a glass conservatory,
Among the orange groves, breathing tropical dreams.

You can use anything as your repetition word. Try using 'like' (it will fit in with the subject of this chapter). You could begin with 'My love is like a red, red rose'. Yes I know, but Burns is a long time out of copyright. Then you might go on to describe all the other things your love is like, getting more and more fantastic as you go on. Or perhaps you could begin 'My dislike/hate (of what, who?) is like'. Here is my passage of anaphora:

Like the secret agony of Geri Halliwell,
Like a century by Geoffrey Boycott,
Like a Rumanian film without subtitles,
Like an anthem for massed choirs by Stockhausen
(Except that nothing could be quite like that)

What is like all that? A poetry reading, of course!

7. Patterning

Rhyme is one kind of patterning and metre is another. You can have metre without rhyme – Shakespearian blank verse for instance; you can have rhyme without metre – Ogden Nash for instance; and you can have poetry without either – free verse.

But, as TS Eliot said, no verse is ever really free. There should be a principle somewhere, though it does not have to be a metric or rhyming principle.

> Twelve for the twelve apostles
> Eleven for the eleven who went to heaven
> Ten for the Ten Commandments
> Nine for the nine bright shiners
> Eight for the April Rainers
> Seven for the seven stars in the sky and
> Six for the six proud walkers
> Five for the symbol at your door and
> Four for the Gospel Makers.
> Three, three the rivals
> Two, two the lilywhite boys, clothed all in green, hallo
> One is one and all alone and evermore shall be so

As a child, I had only a hazy idea of what this meant; it was a good example of Coleridge's observation, that poetry works best when imperfectly understood. I knew it was Christianity of course. My father was assiduous in packing me off to church and Sunday school, perhaps to my moral improvement but certainly to my good as a poet. There are many patterns here – internal rhyme, stress metre, assonance, etc. – but the principal patterning device is number. I know you can think of other poems that fit into this category, right down to the seven men, six men, five men, four men, three men, two men, one man and his dog who all (phew!) went to mow a meadow.

Exercise 9: The poetry of lists

This is from a poem by David Ogston (a Presbyterian Minister actually):

> A tall man
> Stood in the square of darkness,
> Shaking his cloak.
> Out of it fell stars and swords,
> Battered trumpets and candlesticks,
> A fine rain of oatmeal, nails,
> Rules, definitions, ifs and therefores,
> Books in every language.

He mixes up things that could have fallen from a cloak:

> A fine rain of oatmeal, nails

with things that are (surely?) too big:

> Battered trumpets and candlesticks

Two things:

> stars and swords

are entirely different, both in size and in other ways, yoked together through alliteration. The last lines are visually imposs-ible – how would you *draw* that?

> Rules, definitions, ifs and therefores,
> Books in every language.

The list sets up a puzzle, a riddle. What sort of a man would be carrying around a collection of things like this? What are they *for*?

Think of a (magical?) cloak or coat or pocket or bag or box or case or chest belonging to someone (also magical?) and list the things in it. Ogston's man is 'The Storyteller'. Who – or what? – is your person?

Repetitions

One thing I learned from my teachers at school was not to repeat myself. However, that's something a poet must unlearn; repetition is central to poetry. When you repeat something you change it, even if the words are the same. In 'The Hunting of the Snark' Lewis Carroll says, 'What I tell you three times is true!' He is right.

'This is the way the world ends', says TS Eliot three times. The repetitions build up tension, expectation and suspense, making the final 'Not with a bang but with a whimper'... all the more whimpery.

> O whistle an' I'll come to ye, my lad!
> O whistle an' I'll come to ye, my lad!
> Tho' father an' mother an a' should gae mad,
> O whistle an' I'll come to ye, my lad!

The girl in the Burns song feels a love so fierce and all-embracing, a love that cares so little for what the rest of the world thinks or says or does, that is so unchanging, she simply restates it again and again. Can't you hear her driving her parents mad!

Of course the repetition does not have to be exact, nor does it have to be of the whole line. 'Tichborne's Elegy' was 'written with his own hand in the Tower before his execution'. It contains no extraordinary or unusual thought, nor any extraordinary or unusual image either (they are all stock Elizabethan) and there is is no unfolding argument, simply a reiteration in slightly different words. Chidiock Tichborne wrote no other extant poems – he died very young. I have put the repetitions in heavy type:

> **My** prime of youth **is but** a frost of cares,
> **My** feast of joy **is but** a dish of pain,
> **My** crop of corn **is but** a field of tares,
> And all my good **is but** vain hope of gain;
> The day is past, **and yet** I saw no sun,
> **And now** I live, **and now** my life is done.
>
> **My** tale was heard **and yet** it was not told,
> **My** fruit is fallen, **and yet** my leaves are green;
> **My** youth is spent **and yet** I am not old,
> I saw the world **and yet** I was not seen.
> **My** thread is cut **and yet** it is not spun,
> **And now** I live **and now** my life is done.

I sought my death **and** found it in my womb,
I looked for life **and** saw it was a shade,
I trod the earth **and** knew it was my tomb,
And now I die, **and now** I was but made;
My glass is full, **and now** my glass is run,
And now I live, **and now** my life is done.

He wrote this in 1586. This next example dates from the 1950s:

I am the girl who does know better but.
I am the king of the pool.
I am so wise I had my mouth sewn shut.
I am a government official & a goddamned fool.
I am a lady who takes jokes.

The opening stanza of John Berryman's '22nd Dream Song' has metre and rhyme but the patterning device you notice first is simple repetition (anaphora, as we learned in the last chapter). It is a chant, a prayer, a riddle. The repetition insists there is a meaning to be found, even if we have not found it *yet*.

I am a wind of the sea
I am a wave of the sea
I am a sound of the sea
I am a stag of seven tines
I am a griffon on a cliff
I am a tear of the sun

'The Song of Amergin' was, according to Robert Graves, 'chanted by the chief bard of the Milesian invaders as he set foot on the soil of Ireland in the year of the world 2736 (1268 BC)'. So 'I am' songs go back a long way. I wonder if Berryman read 'The White Goddess'. Probably he did.

Exercise 10: I am the great bow-bender

No-one likes a boaster
And I'm not one to boast
But everyone who knows me knows that
I'm the most.

Compose your own 'I am' poem and make it as boastful as possible. The boasting poet is in a long tradition, if that makes you feel better. Make your boasts as outrageous as you can.

> I must be bigger certainly, but that is no great matter;
> An implant of vanadium rods into thighs and upper arms
> Lends the required rigidity for an optimum weight of, say,
> 32 stone plus a good 100lbs for decorations –
> Victoria Cross, Iron Cross, Silver Star, Croix de Guerre,
> Grand Cross of the order of Matthew, Mark, Luke and John . . .

This departs from the model of repeated 'I am's. You can do that too, but you may prefer to stick more closely to the formula, at least initially. The important thing is to be out-rageous. Do you have to tell the truth? Of course you don't. But the most satisfying boasting has some relation to the truth. If it is not what we are, then it is what we wish to be. So boast outrageously for at least ten lines, make it 20 if you can. A good strategy is to write your first draft quite quickly, say in about 15 minutes. If you stop to think too much then you may never tell the lie that is really true. Ted Hughes said that poets were always trying to outwit their internal police system – in other words, that the person you should really try to outrage is yourself. Here is my own attempt at outraging myself – all my life I've wanted to be a bad boy, but alas, I've been too meekly good and now it's too late:

> I am the boy with his feet turned in,
> I am the boy with the golden grin,
>
> The boy with a limp and a crooked tongue;
> If you like me now you won't like me long.
>
> Tickle your arse with a peacock's feather.
> I am the boy with a tart for a mother,
>
> I bring you a song and a broken heart,
> A paper crown and a starry coat.
>
> The only Emperor of Love,
> The boy your father warned you of.
>
> Kiss and tell. Kiss and tell.
> I am the boy who told.

What follows fairly obviously from this is the 'You are...' poem. 'You are the promised breath of springtime' grows into a love poem. (The opposite grows into a hate poem, well worth writing too.) Most love poems are outrageous; their currency is exaggeration and lying. 'You're the Colosseum, the Louvre Museum...' sang Cole Porter, going over the top. Shakespeare played with the idea in his sonnet:

> My mistress eyes are nothing like the sun
> Cherries are much more red than her lips red.
> If snow be white, why then her breasts are dun.
> If hairs be wires, black wires grow on her head.

Gentlemen, then as now, prefer blondes! Write a love poem of exaggeration – they seem to work best this way. Remembering that this is the 21st century (as if we could forget it!) you can bring your images up to date as Auden did in his 'Elegy':

> Let aeroplanes circle moaning overhead
> Scribbling on the sky the message He is Dead,
> Put crepe bows round the white necks of the public doves,
> Let the traffic policemen wear black cotton gloves.

One form of patterning which enables a secret message to be passed – something central to communication between lovers – is the *acrostic*. It often spells out the name of the beloved, but can be used for more underhand purposes. Oliver St John Gogarty (that's 'stately, plump' Buck Mulligan of *Ulysses*) contributed 'The Gallant Irish Yeomen' to what seems to have been an Irish version of *The Tatler*. The poem, ostensibly in praise of Irish soldiers fighting in the Boer War, spelled out a scandalously different message (THE WHORES WILL BE BUSY) in the initial letters of each line. I thought of Gogarty and composed 'Valentine' which amuses children (and me too).

> Wonderfully
> Handsome
> Attractively
> Tanned
>
> Amazingly

Brilliant
Incredibly
Grand

Dearly
Adorable
Fearlessly
True

Witty
And
Loveable
Lusciously
YOU!

Exercise 11: The acrostic me

Write an acrostic poem using your own name. Do not worry, at least initially, about rhyme and scansion; make it a free verse poem. The subject is autobiographical and the initial letters of the lines will spell out your name.

I cannot leave the subject of reiteration/repetition without a word about the poetry of Dylan Thomas. Incantatory repetition is at the very centre of Thomas' art. 'Fern Hill', a poem I find it difficult to read without bursting into tears (so I don't read it – not in public, anyway), is bound together by reiterated words: green, golden, house, farm, light, high, white, young; and phrases: 'young and easy', 'the mercy of his means', 'happy as the . . . was . . .'. Thomas, notoriously, did not worry overmuch about the *exact* meaning of what he wrote, and collected lists of impressive words, slotting them into his poems where he thought they sounded good. Many poets will privately admit that their practice is not entirely different. I have constructed more than one poem by playing with a list of rhymes in *The Penguin Rhyming Dictionary*. Sonnets – good sonnets, too – can be written by starting with the rhyme words.

Visual patterning: concrete poetry

If you supposed that concrete poetry was born with the typewriter – the French poet Guillaume Apollinaire's typewriter, to be exact – then you would be wrong. I am looking now at a sonnet set out in the form of a tree and written in the 17th century by William Sylvester – it must have given the printer no end of trouble. One disadvantage of concrete poetry is that you can't read it aloud, not unless everyone in your audience has access to a copy. Another obvious one is that it can't be particularly subtle – everyone has to get it. A strong element in concrete poetry is *surprise* – which doesn't work so well in art, as TL Peacock pointed out, when you come to it for a second time. But there are times when that is just what you may feel like doing.

The novel Jack Nicholson is writing in Kubrick's film *The Shining*, which shockingly consists of the single line 'All work and no play makes Jack a dull boy' repeated over 500 pages of typescript, might be thought of as a kind of concrete poem. It is also proof positive that Nicholson is mad, of course. The very unmad Ian Hamilton Finlay and Edwin Morgan are kings of the concrete poets in the UK. You have to visit Hamilton Finlay's garden in Scotland to see his best work, but Morgan is available in his collected or selected work and I urge you to buy one of these inspiring books.

Concrete poems can perhaps be divided into 'eye poems', which you have to see on the page, and 'ear poems' which you have to hear in performance. Shape poems and the 'thinks bubbles' of *The Beano* (*see* the poem at this chapter's end) are examples of the first kind. Morgan's 'The Song of the Loch Ness Monster' and Les Murray's Bat poem are examples of the second – both in invented language for non-human creatures. I said that Edwin Morgan was inspiring: here is a concrete poem inspired by him:

sea sonnet

```
w
w  e
w  e  ou
w  e  ou        s
w  e  ou        sh
w  e  ou        ish
w  e  ou        wish
w  e  ou        wish  ou
w  e  ou        wish  ou  wa
w  e  ou        wish  ou  wa  o      ea
w  e  ou        wish you  wa  o      ea
when you        wish you  wa  o      ea
when you        wish you  wa  o  the sea
when you dance I wish you a wave of the sea
```

Is 'sea sonnet' an eye or an ear poem? A bit of both, I would hazard. You certainly have to read it out loud to get the proper effect. The rules of this particular game, invented in a slightly different form by Morgan, are either that you should generate the final line bit by bit by suggestive excerpting; or – by writing it upside-down, as it were – that the line gradually fragments into primal chaos. Some lines are obviously more suitable than others.

Exercise 12: Carved in concrete

Try it yourself. A word processor is useful here, but you have to choose your font, because most concrete poetry is designed for the typewriter where each letter takes up the same space on the page.

A poet does not have to buy into the whole concrete experience, just take what he or she needs. Robert Graves ends his poem 'Leaving the Rest Unsaid' in this way:

> So now, my solemn ones, leaving the rest unsaid,
> Rising in air, as on a gander's wing
> At a careless comma,

I suppose it is possible – and I'm sure Graves managed it – to get the effect purely with the voice, but it *is* primarily for the page. Do not forget what Larkin said:

> Hearing a poem, as opposed to reading it on the page, means you miss so much – the shape, the punctuation, the italics, even knowing how far you are from the end . . . I don't like hearing things in public.

IN THE HOUSE OF DESPERATE DAN

BLUB! BLARGH! BLURB! BLAH!
YIPES! YAHOO! YEEEURGH! YAH!
SNIGGER! CHORTLE! HOOT! GUFFAW!
HEE-HEE! HAW-HAW!

BIFF! BOPP! BAM! BLATT!
SPLISH! SPLOSH! SPLUTTER! SPLAT!
SQUIRT! SQUIFFY! SQUAWK! SQUEAK!
OOOH! AAAH! UURGH! EEEEK!

ROAR! RUMBLE! RASP! R-R-R-RINGG!
Pokka-pokka-pokka-pokka! PHUT! PING!
SNORT! SNIFFLE! SNURGE! SNURR!
WHIFF! WAFFLE! WHOOSH! WHIRR!

CLINK! CLUNK! CREAK! CRASH!
PLINNNGG! PLUNNGG! BOINNGG! BASH!
WAHAH! WAHEY! KERPOW! KERTHUNK!

CLUMP! CLUMP! CLUMP! CLUMP!

OUCH! OOYAH! OOF! OW!
HOLY MACKEREL! HOLY COW!
ZOINKKS! ZAP! ZOWIE! ZOOM!
BEEP-BEEP! VROOM-VROOM!

BOOM!

8. Counting Your Feet – Poetic Metre

Verse in the 20th century has largely escaped the straitjacket of traditional metrics.

So says *The Oxford Companion to English Literature*. But it's not true, though some of my contemporaries have supposed – perhaps even hoped – that it were.

My schools taught me verbs and nouns and clause analysis. Then the Movement For Getting Rid of Grammar told us there were no such things in English – they had all been imported from Latin. Generations of children grew into adults who did not know a noun from a hole in the ground. Now grammar is making a slow comeback (even clause analysis). The companion Movement For Getting Rid Of Metre is likewise falling out of fashion, and a good thing too. You *can* write a poem and know nothing of metrics, just as you *can* play a piano and be unable to read music. But why choose ignorance? Knowledge of metrics may not make a poet out of you – but it will teach you to versify and that is a skill worth having.

Rhythm and metre

We must distinguish between *metre* and *rhythm*. Most poetry has metre, but *all* spoken language has rhythm. Winston Churchill famously offered the British people 'blood, toil, tears and sweat', three heavy stresses, a light one and a final heavy one – the phrase is all hard labour. In the much-heard misquotation 'blood, sweat and tears' – which is also the name of a band – the toil has gone and the phrase positively dances along.

Different languages have different natural rhythms. Michael Bentine used to play a game with a friend when he was a boy. They would converse animatedly in a nonsense which had the rhythms (as they understood them) of Russian, a language neither of them knew. According to Bentine, they were so good at it that native-speaking Russians were deceived – they supposed the boys were indeed speaking their language even if the actual words were unclear. Professor Stanley Unwin used to, and perhaps still does, practise a similar trick in English:

> Oh the self destructibold of the human beale, while we dig in the pokky for a ringside seal towards his fateful and cheer for a bashy-ho. Tutty tutty.

The comic effect depends in great part on his conversational rhythms. If words like 'destructibold' are not English, they sound as if they ought to be. English rhythms depend upon the stress patterns. What do I mean by stress?

Stress

All English utterances of more than one syllable have a pattern of stresses. Two-syllable words will stress on the first, like this:

> random, access, cardboard, parcel, yellow, easy, London, teabag

or on the second, like this:

> install, exhale, perform, entire, compute, prestige

Words in the first list tend to be nouns and adjectives; words in the second list are often verbs. Some words stress differently depending on whether they are nouns or verbs:

> export, record, discard are nouns, but export, record, discard are verbs

Longer words can have more than one stress:

> necessarily, interplanet'ry, antidisestablishment/arianism

Usually there is a primary (main) stress in a long word:

> /   /
> necessarily, interplanet'ry

Different groups of speakers disagree about stress. For example in the US the herb is oregano, but in Britain we say oregano. All the following words are commonly pronounced differently on different sides of the Atlantic:

> US: aristocrat, address, enquiry, research, resource, harass
> UK: aristocrat, address, enquiry, research, resource, harass

Here in Britain Hilaire Belloc rhymed 'harassed' with 'embarrassed' as Robert Frost, say, could not. Contrariwise, Americans Ogden Nash and Theodore Roethke can rhyme 'fertile' with 'turtle' and 'futile' with 'tootle' – fine US rhymes, but no good over here. Southern English speakers collapse the syllables of certain words.

> interplanet'ry (five syllables), diction'ry (three syllables), p'lice (one syllable)

This is thought sloppy by Northeners and Scots, but it is just a speech habit to be seen at its most extreme in the pronunciation of names and places:

> Cholmondeley (Chumly), Gloucester (Gloster), etc.

Americans do not appear to do this much; nor do all English people. The inhabitants of Cirencester pronounce it as it is spelt and do not say 'Sissester' at all. There is a tendency – regrettable, no doubt – for younger people to pronounce words in the US manner which has probably got something to do with television. None of this is set in stone (I say 'harass' in the American manner). Some words used to be pronounced differently. Lines in Browning's 'Soliloquy in a Spanish Cloister' puzzled me:

> I the Trinity illustrate,
> Drinking watered orange pulp –
> In three sips the Arian frustrate;
> While he drains his at one gulp.

Browning's scansion seemed awry until I realised that he pronounced the words 'illustrate' and 'frustrate' as 'illustrate' and 'frustrate' where you and I pronounce them 'illustrate' and 'frustrate'. And if Browning rhymes 'pages' and 'greengages' he must pronounce 'green**gages**' with a stress on the last syllable and not the first as I do. Richard II's, 'A little, little grave, an obscure grave,' and Othello's, 'One whose subdued eyes,' must be pronounced '**ob**scure' and '**sub**dued' in the Elizabethan manner or they will not scan. The stress pattern of a word may be slightly altered in certain contexts. When Ira Gershwin's lyric says:

> It **ain't** necessarily so (. / . . / . . /)

the initial stress on 'necessarily' must be soft-pedalled. 'Similar' has three syllables to me, but a famous lyric rhymes it felicitously with 'Himmler'.

Stressed and unstressed syllables

We see that any English utterance has a pattern of stresses with some syllables stressed and some not. Scansion – marking the metre – of verse ignores the relative *strength* of these stresses – primary stress, secondary stress and so on – and employs simple binary notation, using the symbols (/) for a stressed syllable and (.) for an unstressed one. Sometimes the same set of words can have different patterns of stress. The sentence 'Who are you?' can be stressed three ways:

> **Who ARE you?** (. / .) Meaning 'You have been deceiving us all this time by making us think you were someone else. But now the cat is out of the bag. So who ARE you?'

> **Who are YOU?** (. . /) Meaning 'You have this high opinion of yourself. You think you are important but really you're not. Who do you think you are, you worm? Who are YOU?'

> **WHO are you?** (/ . .) You hear a disembodied voice at a séance . . . You ask, WHERE are you? It says it is at Waterloo. You ask WHO are you? It says it is the Duke of Wellington.

More often we have no choice. When the professor said, 'Faculty library's higgledy-piggledy,' she said it like this:

> **Faculty library's higgledy piggledy.** (/ . . / . . / . . / . .)

70

A line of verse made up of four recurring units (/ . .). She might even have continued:

> Faculty library's higgledy-piggledy.
> None of the books has been catalogued properly.
> Paradise Lost is in Indian Cookery.
> Biblical studies are next to Monopoly.

When I was a child the TV jingle for Pepsodent toothpaste began with the line: 'You'll wonder where the yellow went', which stresses like this:

> You'll wonder where the yellow went (. / . / . / . /)

They are referring to your newly cleaned teeth and follow it up:

> When you brush your teeth with pep so dent. (. . / . / . / . /)

The same four-stress line, though with an extra unstressed syllable at the beginning. 'Pepsodent' would normally sound more like pepsodent (/ . .), say in the phrase pepsodent toothpaste (/ . . / .); here, the last syllable 'dent' rhymes with 'went' and has a heavier stress than it would normally.

Look at these phrases and identify the stress pattern. I have represented each syllable as a little box and grouped the syllables into words. The Beatles gave 'strawberry' three syllables (straw+ber+ry) even though in common speech there are often only two (straw+bry), so I have represented it as ☐☐☐. Mark each syllable with a (/) for a stress, or a (.) for no stress.

Strawberry Fields for ever	☐☐☐ ☐ ☐ ☐☐
Vladivostok to Manchester	☐☐☐☐ ☐ ☐☐☐
Elvis has left the building	☐☐ ☐ ☐ ☐ ☐☐
This is the house that Jack built	☐ ☐ ☐ ☐ ☐ ☐ ☐

Your answers will probably look like this:

Strawberry Fields for ever	/ . . / . / .
Vladivostok to Manchester	/ . / . . / . .
Elvis has left the building	/ . . / . / .
This is the house that Jack built	/ . . / . / .

You could argue plausibly that in the last example there is an additional heavy stress on **built**, so that we end with two heavy stresses – **Jack built** (/ /). Since we are talking about *spoken* language, we cannot always be certain about stress when our examples are only written down. Different people may stress words in different ways. Kevin Costner's Robin Hood refers to **Nottingham** (/ . /), rather than **Nottingham** (/ . .), and Dionne Warwick's name is **War-wick** (/ /) and not **Warrick** (/ .). When as a child I moved to Edinburgh from London, my new schoolfriends were much amused by my London pronunciation of chauffeur as **sho**fer; they all said sha**foor**. And they would pronounce the name of their native city with anything between two syllables (**Em**bra) and four syllables (**Ed-in-bur**-ra) – I think it depended on how posh they were. I now live in Canterbury which can be, and sometimes is, pronounced **Cam**bry, as Riddley Walker does in Russell Hoban's novel.

Though it is possible to say something made up entirely of heavy stresses – the rowing coach's **In! Out! In! Out!** or the countdown at Houston **Five, four, three, two, one** – most of the time there is this alternation: a heavy stress, then one or more light stresses, then a heavy stress again.

Metre

All spoken utterances have rhythm. A poetic metre is a *set pattern* of rhythms – that is, a set pattern of heavy and light stresses. A 'foot' of verse is a unit containing one stressed syllable with either one or two unstressed ones.

- . / (despise, profane, mistake) is an IAMBIC foot or an IAMB
- / . (vulture, taxi, sacred) is a TROCHAIC foot or a TROCHEE
- . . / (repossess, the phrase 'in a trice') is an ANAPAESTIC foot or an ANAPAEST
- / . . (elephant, crocodile). is a DACTYLIC foot or a DACTYL

There is a fifth possible arrangement:

- . / . (confetti, withstanding) is an AMPHIBRACH

as in this one-line poem 'Saturday Afternoon in the Churchyard':

```
    .      /    .    ./ .. / .. / .. / .
There's too much confetti, confetti, confetti
```

But such lines are generally variations in predominantly dactylic or anapaestic metres. This one is dactylic with an extra syllable at the beginning and a truncated (shortened) foot at the end:

```
(.)    /   .    ./ .. / .. / .
There's too much confetti, confetti, confetti
```

The terms are Greek, because the Romans – who first formulated classical metrics – liked to use Greek when talking about Art, as we use French for cooking and Italian for music. We use Greek words in medicine (pharmacy, physiology) and when we speak of politics or helicopters or tricycles.

A line of metrical English verse is made up of a fixed number of feet of the same kind. This one:

```
1      2      3      4      5
.   /  . /    . /    . / ./
Let's talk of graves and worms and ep i-taphs
```

is an **iambic pentameter** because it is made up of five (Greek *pente*) iambs (. /). Greek prefixes added to the stem 'meter' supply names for any line of verse from one foot up to eight.

1 foot = **mono**meter
2 feet = **di**meter
3 feet = **tri**meter
4 feet = **tetra**meter
5 feet = **penta**meter
6 feet = **hexa**meter
7 feet = **hepta**meter
8 feet = **octo**meter

These can be prefixed by iambic, trochaic, dactylic or anapaestic.

```
/   .   /   .   /   .   /   .
Double, double, toil and trouble
```

is a trochaic tetrameter, having four trochees or trochaic feet. This:

  / . .   /   . . / . . / . .
Woman much missed, how you call to me, call to me

is a dactylic tetrameter (though you have to soft-pedal the word 'much' a bit), like the faculty library verse at the beginning of the chapter. And this:

. . / . .   / . . / . . /
The Assyrian came down like a wolf on the fold
. . / . .   / . . / . . /
And his cohorts were gleaming in silver and gold

is a rhyming couplet of anapaestic tetrameter. What about this?

> For you dream you are crossing the channel and tossing about in a
> steamer from Harwich –
> Which is something between a large bathing machine and a very
> small second-class carriage

Each line has exactly the same pattern:

. .   /   . . / . . / . . / . . / .
For you dream you are crossing the channel and tossing about in
. / .   .   / .
a steamer from Harwich –
. / . . / . . / . / . . . / .
Which is something between a large bathing machine and a very
.   / . .   / .
small second-class carriage

Is it anapaestic heptameter with an unstressed syllable at the end?

. . / . . / . . / . . / . . / . . / . . /(.)

Or it *could* be (dactyls and anapaests are tricky things) a dactylic heptameter with two unstressed syllables at the beginning and a syllable missing in the last foot (the technical name for this is an *analeptic* foot).

(..) / . . / . . / . . / . . / . . / . .   / .

Such rhythms, whether you call them anapaestic or dactylic, are very insistent. Once you get into them it can be quite hard to get out again – perhaps one reason why dactylic and anapaestic lines are staples of light verse. But they often find their ways into trochaic and iambic metres as variations. Look at the first three lines of 'Alphabet Pets'.

> Adam ate his awful aardvark.
> Briony bit her boisterous bear.
> Christopher cuddled his comfortable cat.

Line one is purely trochaic: (/ . / . / . / .). Line two has a dactylic variation in the first foot and, possibly (boisterous or boist'rous?), in the third foot as well: (/ . . / . / . . / .) In line three all the feet except the last are dactylic (/ . . / . . /. . /).

Exercise 13: Zoo story

I do this in primary schools but I've tried it out with adults and it works. Think of as many animals as you can with three-syllable names. It should be easy to come up with at least a dozen. Let me start you off with **elephant** and **crocodile**. Fish and insects are animals.

Have you got your animals? Most of them will be dactylic. Throw out any which are not; **elephant** and **crocodile** are dactylic but **mosquito** and **hyena** are not – they are amphibrachs (. / .). You need eight dactylic animals to arrange on this five-line grid in the spaces I have marked THREE.

What about the spaces I have marked ONE? They are for one-syllable animals – but they must be rhyming animals. The first, second and fifth lines should all rhyme together and the third and fourth should rhyme together. To put it another way, the rhyme scheme is **aabba** (*see* also Chapter Five. Actually you can use two-syllable animals instead, but they must be trochaic and they must rhyme on *both* syllables (eagle, beagle, seagull).

THREE	THREE	ONE
THREE	THREE	ONE
THREE	ONE	
THREE	ONE	
THREE	THREE	ONE

Now, if you have managed to follow these rather convoluted directions, you will have a little poem made up entirely of animals. It will sound something like this (I have used names not animals, but you get the idea):

Angela, Millicent, Zoe,	/ . . / . . / .
Imogen, Dorothy, Chloe,	/ . / . . / . .
Charlotte, Charmaine,	/ . . /
Elizabeth, Jane,	. / . . /
Juliet, Jacqueline, Joey.	/ . . / . . / .

What I have written is a limerick of girls' names, and what you will have written is a limerick of animals' names. I have cheated on my original instructions in lines 3 and 4. Line 3 has two names of two syllables each but the stress pattern in unchanged. Line 4 has an extra, unstressed syllable at the front, but it doesn't matter. If you think of the metre as *basically* dactylic, each line can end with a single stress (one syllable), a trochee (two syllables) or a dactyl (three syllables). And it can easily incorporate up to two unstressed syllables at the beginnings of the lines. In the following limerick I have bracketed those 'extra' syllables at the front:

> (There) was a young lady of Tottenham
> (Who'd no) manners, or else she'd forgotten 'em;
> (Taking) tea at the vicar's
> (She) tore off her knickers
> (Be)cause, she explained, she felt hot in 'em.

This could also be scanned anapaestically, like all limericks. I was writing verse in these patterns long before I knew the names. How did I do it? I copied. I wrote a love song:

> Jenny Jefferey! I loved you with a lonely passion when,
> With our turned-up raincoat collars and our Woodie packs of ten,
> Our lot drank Skol Lager in Milne's Bar and hoped we looked like men.

The tripping trochaic metre is from Browning's 'A Toccata of Galuppi's'.

> As for Venice and its people, merely born to bloom and drop,
> Here on earth they bore their fruitage, mirth and folly were the
>   crop:
> What of life was left, I wonder, when the kissing had to stop?

Poets who like such metrical fireworks include Browning, Hardy, Auden, Betjeman, Gavin Ewart and James Fenton. And WS Gilbert and Lewis Carroll, if you count them as poets – which I certainly do. There are no women on that list; perhaps the show-off style is more a male thing.

Parody

A parody is a pastiche (imitation) of a literary style done for comic effect. One of my favourites is 'Brahma' by Andrew Lang, parodying Ralph Waldo Emerson. A stanza of Emerson first:

> If the red slayer thinks he slays,
>   Or if the slain thinks he is slain,
> They know not well the subtle ways
>   I keep, and pass, and turn again

Now Lang:

> If the wild bowler thinks he bowls,
>   Or if the batsman thinks he's bowled,
> They know not, poor misguided souls,
>   They too shall perish unconsoled.
>
> I am the batsman and the bat,
>   I am the bowler and the ball,
> The umpire, the pavilion cat,
>   The roller, pitch and stumps and all.

As with Lewis Carroll's parodies of now-forgotten models by Southey and Isaac Watts, this poem stands on its own. A parody does not have to be critical of its source. Philip Larkin's 'This Be The Verse' – the one that begins 'They fuck you up, your mum and dad' – has spawned many imitations, including 'They tuck you up' (Simon Rae) and 'They buck you up' (me), more by way of tribute than criticism. What about Kit Wright's beautiful 'George

Herbert's Other Self In Africa' in Chapter 5? It's good to have parody in your poet's toolkit. Pound's parodies 'Ancient Music' and 'Prayer to Venus' are among his best poems.

The trochaic tetrameter of Longfellow's 'Hiawatha' is a good place to start. Carroll and Ewart have both done it successfully, but my favourite is this, usually classed as one of the many poems written by the great Anon, but actually the work of George A Strong:

> When he killed the Mudjokovis.
> Of the skin he made him mittens,
> Made them with the fur side inside,
> Made them with the skin side outside.
> He, to get the warm side inside,
> Put the inside skinside outside;
> He, to get the cold side outside,
> Put the warm side fur side inside.
> That's why he put the fur side inside,
> Why he put the skin side outside,
> Why he turned them inside outside.

Exercise 14: Hiawatha makes a cup of tea

> Boil the water in a kettle.
> Put a teabag in a mug and
> Pour the boiling water on it.
> Stir the tea round with a teaspoon
> Fish the teabag from the water.
> Throw it in the rubbish basket
> Add the milk and add the sugar
> Stir again and drink with pleasure.

Describe some everyday task – making a phone call, boiling an egg, cleaning your teeth – in the Hiawatha metre (which is trochaic tetrameter, since you ask).

Exercise 15: Song lyrics

Try some new lyrics to an old song. You can either do what Noel Coward did when he added new verses to Cole Porter's 'These Foolish Things', or you can write lyrics in direct opposition to the original, like these:

Bring me breath like rotten cheese;
Bring me darkness and disease...

Or your lyrics can have a loose thematic connection. My
Christmas Carol:

Come to our Nativity Play,
Raggy doll asleep in the hay,
Itchy knickers, bogey pickers,
I've got a bit to say.

goes, I hope obviously, to the tune of 'We Three Kings of
Orient'. You can always sing your lyrics to make sure you've
got the metre right – children do it all the time. I remember my
Primary School friend, Colin Bryce, singing his version of
'Robin Hood, Robin Hood, Riding through the glen':

Junior Robin, Junior Robin,
Running down the street,

I could quote (though I won't) lavatorial versions of Davy
Crockett, Country Gardens and practically any song by The
Spice Girls. Kit Wright's 'Worried Man Blues' and 'The Orbison
Consolations' are worth looking up.

9. Blank Verse and Free Verse

'Blank verse', says the poet Philip Hobsbaum, 'is the metre in which most of the great poetry has been written.' I wouldn't quarrel with that. What is verse? What makes it blank?

Poetry, verse and rhyme

Words are elusive. They mean different things in different times and in different places. Up to about a 100 years ago most people would have agreed that most *poetry* was written in *verse*, meaning it had a consistent metrical pattern. Some people whose opinions are worth listening to – for instance the poet John Hollander – still think so. Everyone agrees with Johnson (*see* Chapter 2) that not all verse is poetry.

> Thirty days have September,
> April, June and November.
> All the rest have thirty-one
> Excepting February alone,
> Which has twenty-eight days clear
> And twenty-nine in each leap year.

Mnemonics like this are written in rhymed verse or *rhyme* for short, in order to make them more easily remembered, but they are not poetry.

> Western wind, when wilt thou blow
> That the small rain down can rain?
> Christ, that my love were in my arms
> And I in my bed again.

This is verse too; it is also poetry.

> Ride a Cock Horse
> To Banbury Cross
> To see a fine lady
> Upon a white horse

Poetry? I say so, but to some it is no more than a Nursery Rhyme. Is Ogden Nash a poet or just a versifier? I know what I think, but I also know that these are matters of opinion not fact.

All the verse I have so far quoted is in rhyme also, but verse does not have to rhyme. The times tables which children used to chant, and perhaps still do in privileged schools, are in unrhymed verse with a regular metre:

> Two twos are four
> Three twos are six
> Four twos are eight ...

The commonest kind of unrhymed metrical verse in English is *blank verse*, which is where we came in.

Blank verse

This is from Christopher Marlowe's *Dr Faustus*:

> Was this the face that launched a thousand ships, and burned the topless towers of Ilium? Sweet Helen, make me immortal with a kiss! Her lips suck forth my soul; see, where it flies! Come Helen, come, give me my soul again.

And this from William Shakespeare's *Richard II*:

> Let's talk of graves, of worms and epitaphs, make dust our paper, and with rainy eyes write sorrow on the bosom of the earth. Let's choose executors and talk of wills. And yet not so – for what can we bequeath, save our deposed bodies to the ground?

I have written them as prose (in other words as not-verse), but it is not too difficult to see where the line-breaks come, particularly if you read them aloud. Begin the first passage with this line:

> Was this the face that launched a thousand ships

And the second with this:

> Let's talk of graves and worms and epitaphs

You must take care to say 'launcht' in passage 1 where you are Dr

Faustus, but depose**d** in passage 2 where you are King Richard. This last is a pronunciation Shakespeare could allow himself but we cannot, though poets went on doing it – old-fashioned things that they were and are – till well into the 19th century. Each one of these lines has five stresses:

. / . / . /   . /   .   /
Was this the face that launched a thousand ships

.   / . /   .   /   . / ./
Let's talk of graves and worms and epitaphs

As Hobsbaum said, most great English poetry is written in blank verse. Perhaps because it is the metre closest to natural speech: Shakespeare's plays (and the plays of all the other Elizabethans and Jacobeans), 'Paradise Lost', Wordsworth's 'Prelude', fine poems by Coleridge, Keats, Tennyson, Matthew Arnold, TS Eliot, John Betjeman – the list goes on. Dickens, a keen amateur actor, fell into a kind of blank verse when he was pulling out all the emotional stops in those purple passages which set the Victorians a-sobbing and which we find so hard to take. (Oscar Wilde, a modern in this respect, said you would need a heart of stone not to laugh at the death of Little Nell.) I stumbled on a fine, booming rendition of Dickens as I was re-tuning my car radio; it formed part of an anthology of JK Rowling's favourite literary passages. I have set it out *as if it were poetry*, which is the way I heard it.

> I see the lives for which I lay down my life,
> Peaceful, useful, prosperous and happy,
> In that England which I shall see no more.
> I see her with a child upon her bosom
> Who bears my name. I see her father,
> Aged and bent, but otherwise restored
> And faithful to all men in his healing office
> And at peace.
> I see the good old man, so long their friend,
> In ten years time enriching them with all
> He has,
> And passing tranquilly to his reward.

Not *quite* blank verse but nearly. I think it's a bit ham – Dickens hammed up readings of his works to terrific effect and I'm sure he did this as a barnstorming, bravura piece. It is from the end of *A Tale of Two Cities* – Sidney Carton's thoughts as his tumbrel rolls to the guillotine.

Shakespeare often turned someone else's prose into his blank verse. Sir Thomas North's translation of the Greek, Plutarch:

> ... she disdained to set forward otherwise, but to take her barge on the river of Cydnus; the poop whereof was of gold, the sails of purple and the oars of silver, which kept stroke in rowing after the sound of musicke of flutes, howboys, citherns, viols and such other instrumenst as they played upon the barge. And now for the person of herself; she was laid under a pavilion of cloth of gold of tissue, apparelled and attired like the goddess Venus commonly drawn in picture: and hard by her, on either hand of her, pretty fair boys, apparelled as painters do set forth the god Cupid, with little fans in their hands with which they fanned upon her. Her Ladies and Gentlewomen ...

Shakespeare versifies it thus:

> The barge she sat in, like a burnish'd throne
> Burned on the water: the poop was beaten gold;
> Purple the sails, and so perfumed that
> The winds were love-sick with them; the oars were silver,
> Which to the tune of flutes kept stroke, and made
> The water which they beat to follow faster,
> As amorous of their strokes. For her own person,
> It beggar'd all description: she did lie
> In her pavilion – cloth of gold of tissue –
> O'er picturing that of Venus, where we see
> The fancy outwork nature: on each side of her
> Stood pretty, dimpled boys, like smiling Cupids,
> With divers-coloured fans, whose wind did seem
> To glow the delicate cheeks which they did cool,
> And what they undid did.
> Her gentlewomen, like the Nereides ...

Of course, he makes *great* poetry; but it's interesting, nevertheless, to see how much magpie Shakespeare stole. Bad poets borrow, good poets steal, as Eliot (and Alexander Pope before him) said. There is even such a thing as a 'found' poem, as we shall see.

Johnson, who disliked blank verse and did not write it well, in

common with his age, said that it 'is verse only to the eye'. Sometimes, certainly – the Victorian, George Eveleigh, wrote this (and
yes, he was serious):

> Thus, if a Government agrees to give,
> Whenever Public Companies are formed,
> To each a dividend – say six per cent
> Per annum for a certain fixed time,
> And for security inspects accounts . . .

and so on. Poets have solved this problem of prosey blank verse in
different ways. Milton constructed huge paragraphs with a convoluted syntax that he borrowed from Latin. This is the opening
sentence of 'Paradise Lost'.

> Of Man's First Disobedience, and the fruit.
> Of that Forbidden Tree, whose mortal taste
> Brought Death into the World and all our woe,
> With loss of Eden, till one greater Man
> Restore us and regain the blissful seat

It *is* like Latin; we are still waiting for the verb.

> Sing,

At last! But who is to sing?

> Heavenly Muse, that on the secret top
> Of Horeb or of Sinai didst inspire
> That Shepherd

What Shepherd?

> who first taught the chosen seed,
> In the beginning how the Heaven and Earth
> Rose out of chaos:

The shepherd is Moses . . .

> or if Sion hill
> Delight thee more, and Siloa's brook that flow'd
> Fast by the Oracle of God;

And that's King David (or at least it's the person who wrote the

Psalms) . . .

> I thence
> Invoke their aid to my adventurous Song.
> That with no middle flight intends to soar
> Above th'Aonian Mount,

Mount Helicon where the Muses of Homer and Virgil lived . . .

> while it pursues
> Things unattempted yet in Prose or Rhyme.

A sentence of 16 lines is not at all unusual for Milton – highly wrought and hardly verse 'only to the eye'. If you wish to take this fascinating (to me) subject further, then look up the passage near the beginning of Book Three, where Milton alliterates the words fall, faithless, fault, free, fall, failed, fell, free – all within the space of eight lines.

The very un-Miltonic Tennyson, in his 'Ulysses', similarly *enjambs* his lines (runs the sense across the line-endings). Just look at all those chiming 's', 'z' and 'r' sounds:

> Life piled on life
> Were all too little, and of one to me
> Little remains: but every hour is saved
> From that eternal silence, something more,
> A bringer of new things; and vile it were
> For some three suns to store and hoard myself,
> And this gray spirit yearning in desire
> To follow knowledge like a sinking star,
> Beyond the utmost bound of human thought.

Wallace Stevens goes further; his blank verse hovers on the very edge of rhyme. 'Sunday Morning' is written in 15-line stanzas that remind us of sonnets, with chiming consonants (in heavy type) instead of rhyme, and repetition (underlined).

> Supple and turbulent, a ring of **men**
> Shall <u>chant</u> in orgy on a **summer morn**
> Their boisterous devotion to the **sun**,
> Not <u>as a god</u>, but <u>as a god</u> might be,
> Naked among them, like a savage **source**.
> Their <u>chant</u> shall be a <u>chant</u> of para**dise**,
> Out of their blood, returning to the **sky**;
> And in their <u>chant</u> shall enter, voice by voi**ce**,

The windy lake wherein their lord delights,
There really is very little danger of mistaking *that* for chopped-up prose, though it is true that much of the prose of the 16th and 17th centuries used similar devices (Donne and Milton spring to mind).

John Betjeman's language is quite different. In his autobiographical 'Summoned by Bells' he plays amusingly with 'unpoetic' material (fish glue) and 'unpoetic' words ('Stickphast' and 'laundriness').

> Evening brought back the gummy smell of toys
> And fishy stink of glue and Stickphast paste,
> And sleep inside the laundriness of sheets

The verse itself is heavily end-stopped – the opposite of enjambed – and very regular metrically. It has to be; if you don't use a 'high' style then you have to keep the metre tight. You have to be witty too, or you will fall as clumsily into Johnson's trap as Mr Eveleigh did.

Exercise 16: Prose into verse

Do what Shakespeare did. Take a piece of prose, from a book or from a newspaper, and turn it into blank verse. It will be easy because the rhythms are already there. This is from the *Daily Telegraph*, tweaked a bit, but not much:

> Bob Ayling, former Chairman of the Dome
> Said people were 'pathetic' when they knocked
> Millennium projects. 'It's like a disease,'
> He said, 'the way the British Press set up
> Aunt Sallies and then knock them down again'.

Free verse

The poet who wants more freedom and with it a looser, more throwaway line, needs something else. Free verse! Can there be such a thing? Isn't the whole point of verse that it is constrained by metre? But the term is nevertheless used and understood. The 50-word poem I produced – as did you, I hope – in Chapter 1 was in free verse.

The beautiful girl in the flowing white dress struggled along the platform at the Angel. In one hand she carried, a large suitcase. In the other, another. On reaching me she stopped. Green eyes flashing like stolen butterflies. 'Would you be so kind as to carry one for me,' she asked, 'as far as Bank?' I laughed. 'My pleasure.' And it was. Safe from harm, all the way to Bank, moist in my palm, one green eye.

'Laughing all the way to Bank' is a complete poem by Roger McGough. Can you break it up into lines? It is not quite so easy as with blank verse, is it? What rule can you go by? Suppose you fix on a two-stress line. Your poem might begin this way:

The **beautiful girl**
In the **flowing** white **dress**
Struggled along
The **plat**form at the **Angel**

Or perhaps you might try a syllabic pattern:

the beautiful girl in	6
the flowing white dress	5
struggled along the	5
platform at the Angel	6

In neither of these cases could the verse be said to be 'free', and in fact McGough does something quite different. Suppose I tell you that it is a poem in five stanzas, the first of four lines, the next three of three lines each and the last of four lines again. Can you do it now? Suppose I write out the first stanza for you.

The beautiful girl
in the flowing white dress
struggled along the platform
at the Angel

This is McGough's arrangement. But why not like this?

The beautiful girl in
the flowing white dress
struggled
along the platform at
the Angel

Is his arrangement really better? I think so. *His* first line focuses us on the beautiful girl, whereas mine makes us wonder, irrelevantly, exactly what it was she was in – the bus, a temper, my dreams? And when I give 'struggled' a line to itself I give it more attention than it deserves. The most important thing in the stanza becomes her struggle rather than her beauty. And is there any reason, in my penultimate line, to keep us in suspense about the name of the tube station? To sum it up: my lineation is idiosyncratically inept, where McGough's is quiet and natural. When, in the second stanza, he does employ an unusual line-break – along with some Shakespearean commas, by which I mean they are there to aid the voice rather than the sense – it helps us to hear a particular tone, which we *must* hear if the poem is to work.

> In one hand
> she carried, a large suitcase.
> In the other, another

McGough's poem is a poem by Coleridge's definition: 'the best words *in the best order*' (my italics). But we *could* defend line-breaks at other places. When God is dead, as Nietzsche observed, everything is permitted. If you play tennis without a net and lines on a court, as my children used to on the road outside our house, then how do you decide who has won a point? My sister invented one wet afternoon a kind of Scrabble where only words that didn't exist were allowed. You will be unsurprised to learn that it didn't catch on. Once verse becomes 'free' then a certain pleasure is lost, the pleasure Robert Louis Stevenson was talking about when he said that in verse he expected something and he got it. In free verse we never know quite what to expect so we never quite know whether we have got it or not. McGough's poem gets by on a verbal ambiguity, felicitous phrasing and charm. DH Lawrence called free verse 'organic form'. He called his own free-verse poems 'Pansies', a self-deprecating joke (Pascale's *Pensées* + a kind of limp-wristed poetic ineffectualness – homophobic Lawrence's joke, not mine). His free verse is witty and epigrammatic. It is light verse.

The history of free verse

Free verse in a translation from the French *vers libre*. French versification was/is subject to more stringent rules than English, and consequently the desire to escape was more pronounced. *Vers libre* was invented by the great poet-prodigy Arthur Rimbaud towards the end of the 19th century. Or it was invented by the nearly-as-great poet Laforgue, and imported into Britain a few years later. Or we got it from Walt Whitman, the American poet who was writing well before Rimbaud. Or from Christopher Smart's 'Jubilate Deo', a century further back:

> For I will consider my cat Jeoffry.
> For he is the servant of the living god duly and daily serving him.
> For at the first glance of the glory of God in the East he worships in his way.
> For is this done by wreathing his body seven times round with elegant quickness.

Or from the Bible. Both Whitman and Smart knew the Authorised Version:

> Surely there is a mine for silver,
> And a place for gold which they refine.
> Iron is taken out of the earth
> And brass is molten out of the stone,
> And searcheth out to the furthest bound
> The stones of thick darkness and of the shadow of death.

This is from the 28th chapter of the Book of Job. Whitman's practice is similar:

> I celebrate myself
> And what I assume you shall assume
> For every atom belonging to me, as good as belongs to you

In a less lofty tone, perhaps whimsically, for free verse does attract whimsy, one might write:

> A paddleboat
> on the Vierwaldstattersee
> as the Lake of Lucerne should
> properly be called,
> is Titlis

> 'Honest,' says Kickoff, jumping up and down.

The problem of *where the lines should properly begin* is a real one. I can see no particular reason why, in the last example, 'A paddleboat' should have a line to itself and, say, 'jumping up and down' should not.

Exercise 17: Line-endings

Here is a 'One-Sentence Poem'. It is written in three stanzas of six, five and six lines as indicated. Where would you put the line breaks?

> When Esmeralda grew up she hung up her childhood on a tree, she hung up her childhood like an old red dress while all the grown-ups cried, 'Too small. Too small, Esmeralda!' though really it was Esmeralda who was too big,

> and her childhood swung in the wind, her childhood swung and turned in the wind, glittering and shining it swung and turned, not just red but orange and yellow and green and blue and violet and gold and silver,

> while all the children cried, 'Come back, come back, Esmeralda!' and Esmeralda turned, swung and turned, swung and turned in the wind like an old red dress.

It certainly does not read like prose. The cadences are too regular, the language is heightened, or at least too repetitive for modern prose. If you break it up into the lines that seem 'organically right', as DH Lawrence might have said, then what you get will probably be similar to the original, but not exactly the same. The 'right' answer is at the end of the chapter.

Exercise 18: 'Found' poetry

Look through a book or a newspaper for a story or a part of a story that you can write out in free verse to make a 'found poem'. The rules are that you may not change anything in the extract except the line-endings. The novel *Agnes Grey* by Anne Brontë begins thus:

> My father was a clergyman, of the North of England, deservedly respected by all who knew him, and in his younger days he lived

pretty comfortably on the joint income of a small incumbency and a snug little property of his own.

This pleasantly rhythmic sentence can be arranged in lines:
>My father was a clergyman
>Of the North of England,
>Who was deservedly respected
>By all who knew him,
>And in his younger days,
>He lived pretty comfortably
>On the joint income
>Of a small incumbency
>And a snug little property of his own.

It now looks like a (free verse?) poem. Does that make it one? If it does, then did I write it, or did Anne Brontë? Was it my act of finding that made the sentence poetry, as Duchamp made a urinal into art (democratic art – anybody can do it) by sticking it up on the wall of a gallery?

Answers to 'line-endings'

Laughing All the Way to the Bank

The beautiful girl
In the flowing white dress
Struggled along the platform
At the Angel.

In one hand
She carried, a large suitcase.
In the other, another.

On reaching me
She stopped. Green eyes flashing
Like stolen butterflies.

'Would you be so kind
as to carry one for me,'
she asked, 'as far as Bank?'

I laughed: 'My pleasure.'
And it was. Safe from harm,
All the way to Bank,
Moist in my palm, one green eye.

One-Sentence Poem

When Esmeralda grew up
She hung up her childhood on a tree.
She hung up her childhood like an old red dress
While all the grown-ups cried,
'Too small. Too small, Esmeralda!'
Though really it was Esmeralda who was too big.

And her childhood swung in the wind.
Her childhood swung and turned in the wind.
Glittering and shining it swung and turned,
Not just red but orange and yellow
And green and blue and violet and gold and silver.

While all the children cried,
'Come back, come back, Esmeralda!' And Esmeralda turned,
Swung and turned,
Swung and turned in the wind
Like an old red dress.

Perhaps your versions were different. Were they inferior? Who is to say? Are you comfortable with the fact that, though there are certainly a lot of wrong answers, there are no right ones? Does free verse have *any* rules? Poets may internalise rules of their own but how do we know what they are? I have no easy answers to these questions. I used to once, but as I get older I get less sure of things, even the difference between poetry and prose.

Free verse is difficult to write well because there is no structure except what you yourself create. So you must *raise* your language from the everyday – it really does have to be 'the best words in the best order'. Otherwise – prose chopped up! If you take my advice you will use free verse sparingly; if you don't you will write badly, and worse, you will be *dull*.

10. Syllabic Verse

English metre counts stresses, but French metre counts syllables – and the Alexandrine line of Racine has 12 syllables rather than a particular number of stresses. Stress is not as important a constituent of any Romance language as it is of English; one of the reasons why we speak French badly, and why a French person speaking English usually gets the stress – the music of the language – wrong and always sounds like Maurice Chevalier.

For about 80 years from the time of Charles II (the Augustan period), English verse was consciously syllabic. The heroic couplets of Dryden and Pope had ten syllables, as well as five stresses. Even the feminine rhyme – which is an extra, unstressed syllable at the end – was rarely employed and 'smoothness' of versification was much praised. Verses were commonly printed like this:

> For our wise Rabble ne'er took pains t'enquire,
> What 'twas he burnt, so't made a rousing fire.

to show just how it accorded with the ten-syllable rule. Dryden smoothed out Chaucer (whose pronunciation was not understood – he is very smooth already); Pope smoothed out Donne; Shakespeare was considered a rustic of genius and Dryden entirely rewrote Anthony and Cleopatra for a more polite age.

Johnson, it is true, scoffed at the too-mechanical 'numbering' of verses:

> I used once to be plagued by a man who wrote verses, but who literally had no other notion of a verse, but that it consisted of ten syllables. *Lay your knife and your fork, across your plate*, was to him a verse.

This man with the tin ear would scan the line thus:

> Lay **your** knife **and** your **fork,** across your **plate**

when the natural speech rhythm is probably this:

> Lay your **knife** and your **fork,** across your **plate** (/ . / . . / . / . /)

Gavin Ewart, inventively, writes a whole poem, 'Leaving Leeds', using this line's rhythm as his metrical norm.

> Lay your knife and your fork, across your plate,
> see the sun as it shines, on yellow egg,
> brighter certainly too, your bacon gone.

Exercise 19: Fascinating rhythms

Ewart's *jeu d'esprit* suggests this exercise. Start with an interesting line that does not seem, on the face of it, to have a metrical feel to it. In a class you could invent one for the person on your right, receiving your own assigned line from your left. Or you might take a newspaper headline. Now write a poem using the rhythm of this line as your metrical norm. 'Leaving Leeds' is 30 lines long, but aim for eight lines to start with. My headline is 'Belgium looks to Britain for laughs':

> Belgium looks to Britain for laughs: (/ . / . / . . /)
> Britain looks to Belgium for what?
> Simenon and Tin-Tin and coal,
> Saxophones and Poirot and sprouts,
> Flemish grit and snobby Walloons.
> Antwerp, Brussels, Mons and Ostend,
> Whoring, warring, boring and ships,
> Belgium looks to Britain for laughs.

English syllabics

Those Belgian verses all have eight syllables but the patterning device is stress not syllable. The pure syllabic poetry in English that has been written in the last 60 years or so depends on the syllabic pattern running *counter* to the stress, so that you get a series of lines of differing stress patterns held together by the (arbitrary?) device of a syllable count. The American poet Marianne Moore is the most interesting of these. Her poetry gets its particular flavour from the way it seems to dip in and out of prose rhythms. WH Auden, Thom Gunn and others have also used syllabics, though they tend to stick to a line of nine or 11 syllables which cannot therefore be mistaken for the iambic pentameter of blank verse. When I try to write 'pure' syllabics I find myself slipping into ordinary patterns of stress-based English verse – which must not happen. Otherwise, why bother?

> O you chorus of indolent reviewers,
> Irresponsible, indolent reviewers,
> Look, I come to the test, a tiny poem
> All composed in a metre of Catullus,
> All in quantity, careful of my motion,
> Like the skater on ice that hardly bears him,
> Lest I fall unawares before the people,
> Waking laughter in indolent reviewers.

Tennyson's 'Hendecasyllabics', written in a classical quantitive metre which, translated into English metrical practice, looks like this.

> / . / . ./ . / . / .
> O you chorus of indolent reviewers

Exercise 20: Eleven syllables

Try writing a poem in 11-syllable lines, either according to pure syllabic practice or in Catullus' metre (as anglicised by me). Call it 'Eleven' and see if that, at first sight, unmagical number, suggests anything to you? One short of a dozen. One more than ten. Players in a football team. 'Elevenses' – a delicate Winnie-the-Pooh-ish name for what Americans crudely call brunch. And don't forget that 'eleven were the eleven who went to heaven'.

> Magic numbers are threes and fives and sevens:
> Wishes, pentagrams, princes and princesses . . .

Stevie Smith begins her 'Hendecasyllables' in the following delicate fashion:

> It is the very bewitching hour of eight
> Which is the moment when my new day begins,

Classical metres in English – hexameters and elegiacs

Strictly you can't do classical metres in English because Greek and Latin metre is based on quantity (the difference between long and short syllables), whereas English metre is based on stress (the difference between stressed and unstressed syllables).

Long and short syllables

The vowel **a** in cat is short; in cart it is long. Similar pairs are met and meet, lit and light, cod and code, plum and plume. Often the long/short vowels coincide with the pattern of stresses, but not always. In Marlowe's line

/   /   /   /   /

Was this the face that launched a thousand ships

this and **ships** are stressed, though the vowels are short. It is *possible* to make stress and length coincide: 'Was **yours** the face that launched a thousand **boats**' would do it, but, alas, the poetry has disappeared. No, you can't do it unless you substitute the English principle (stressed/unstressed) for the classical one (long/short). And this is what poets do.

Dactylic hexameter

Five dactyls, followed by a spondee. What is a spondee? Some two-syllable words in English can have a trochaic (/ .) stress pattern like **random** or **exit**; others have an iambic (. /) stress pattern like **pursue** or **imply**. But a few words, it can be argued, have the stress equally distributed on both syllables. Examples would be **ping-pong**, **jam-jar** and **crossroads**, and it is no accident that two of my examples are hyphenated. It is also true that all these words can be stressed trochaically (/ .) in a line of verse. Here is a hexameter by Longfellow easy to remember as a model:

/ . . / . . / . . / . . / . . / /

This is the forest primeval. The murmuring pines and the hemlocks

A Greek or Latin poet can substitute a spondee (/ /) for any dactyl *except* the last foot before the spondee at the end. In English a trochee will do as well as a spondee, so it comes down to this: an English hexameter is a six-stress line made up of dactyls and trochees, with the last foot always a trochee. These are hexameters from Arthur Hugh Clough's 'Amours de Voyage' – accentual hexameters, he calls them, but *all* good hexameters in English are accentual. I have scanned the first line to let you see how it works:

/ . ./ . / .. / . / .. / .
Whither depart the souls of the brave that die in the battle,
Die in the lost, lost fight, for the cause that perishes with them?
Are they upborne from the field on the slumberous pinions of
    angels .. ?

It all sounds rather 19th century, and of course it is. Peter Reading's hexameters are another matter: he arranges his line-endings differently and allows himself occasional unstressed syllables at the beginnings of lines (e.g. line 3). Each pair of lines is a hexameter, divided after the fourth foot.

Outside Victoria Station a quorum of
    No-hoper foetid
Impromptu imbibers is causing a shindy:
    One of the number,
Clutching a bottle of Thunderbird, half-full,
    Rolls among litter

Elegiac couplets

A hexameter followed by a pentameter of two halves ($2\frac{1}{2}$ feet + $2\frac{1}{2}$ feet) makes an elegiac couplet. This is the pattern:

/ .. / .. /   / .. / .. /
Horrible, horrible hound! Terrible, terrible toad!

According to English metrical rules that is not actually a pentameter, since it has six stresses. Dactyls can be replaced by spondees or trochees:

/ . / . / / . / . /
Ghastly, ghastly goat! Nasty, nasty newt!

Gavin Ewart's 'Advertising Elegiacs' are fun:

/ . / . . / . . / . . / . . / .
Advertising! The men at the front are most terribly turdlike!
  / . / . . / / . . / . . /
Backroom boys are the best; they can be human (a bit).

John Heath-Stubbs's 'Epitaph for Thais' (an Athenian courtesan who accompanied Alexander the Great) is very elegant:

> Neo-Platonic sages failed to show up at their lectures –
>   Dream of the touch of her lips, metaphysics go hang!

English practice allows unstressed syllables between the two halves of the pentameter. These are still elegiacs, according to me:

> Over the back wall and out into the water meadow,
>   Down there by the lake and a big moon shining clear.

Hexameters and elegiacs are a good way of not writing in blank verse.

11. Rhyme, Near-rhyme and Alliteration

How does rhyme work? Most rhymes are like this:

> A man of words and not of **deeds**
> Is like a garden full of **weeds**

Weeds/deeds is a *masculine* rhyme on a single stressed syllable.

> Why did you die when the lambs were **cropping?**
> You should have died at the apples' **dropping,**
> When the grasshopper comes to **trouble,**
> And the wheatfields are sodden **stubble,**
> And all winds go **sighing**
> For sweet things **dying.**

All Christina Rossetti's rhymes are *feminine*; they rhyme on two syllables with the stress pattern (/ .) which means that each line ends on a weak syllable. This kind of rhyme is considered sweeter and more mellifluous, just as the first kind is considered more muscular. Is this terminology sexist? Yes, I'm afraid it is.

You *can* rhyme on more than two syllables. WS Gilbert's Major General rhymes trisyllabically (on three syllables) through a whole song:

> I'm very well acquainted too with matters mathe**matical,**
> I understand equations, both the simple and quad**ratical,**
> About binomial theorem I am teeming with a **lot o' news** –
> With many cheerful facts about the square on the hy**potenuse.**

The ingenious Kit Wright even has a tetrasyllabic set of rhymes in a limerick (**Kidderminster/ridderminster/quidderminster**). The 19th century poet Thomas Hood wrote 'Bridge of Sighs' about a girl abandoned by her family (presumably she was pregnant) found drowned in the Thames.

Alas! For the **rarity**
Of Christian **charity**
   Under the sun!
O, it was **pitiful!**
Near a whole **city full,**
   Home had she none

The effect Hood intended – and got too, for the poem was very popular – is probably no longer possible. Such rhymes seem comic now and an unfunny poem with trisyllabic rhymes is, like a serious limerick (actually attempted by Gavin Ewart), probably doomed to failure – unless you are Thomas Hardy, that is. The first stanza of 'The Voice':

Woman much missed, how you call to me, call to me
Saying that now you are not as you were
When you had changed from the one who was all to me,
But as at first, when our day was fair.

I judged a competition recently, and out of 70 poems from the members of a good local poetry society, only two employed rhyme. Matthew Sweeney and John Hartley Williams in *Writing Poetry and Getting It Published* claim, with some truth, that 'dislike of rhyme in modern writing is ... widespread'. They go on to say that 'ingenuity may have that "Look Ma, no hands!" quality about it that serious poetry ... would do well to avoid'. I am a bit unhappy about that.

I am unhappy too about the term 'light verse' that I used in the last chapter and don't think it should remain unchallenged. As Gavin Ewart pointed out, the opposite of light verse ought to be heavy verse (and, God knows, there is plenty of that), but it is not. The opposite of 'light verse' is 'serious poetry' and light versifiers are not serious people, they are jokers and 'lack bottom' as Johnson might have said. Naturally I dispute this.

But rhyme *has* made a comeback over the last 20 years, at least this side of the Atlantic. Here is a UK XI of habitual rhymers (and 'Look, no hands!' rhymers sometimes, too) – the oldest over 80 and the youngest under 30.

Charles Causley, Tony Harrison, Wendy Cope, Sophie Hannah, John Fuller, James Fenton, Carol Ann Duffy, Simon Rae, Glyn Maxwell, Roger McGough, Vernon Scannell, John Whitworth (drinks waiter)

None (except Sophie Hannah perhaps) uses rhyme all the time, but they do it pretty often. In the USA the rhymers are more embattled (though Anthony Hecht, Dana Gioia and Richard Wilbur are still at it), but the great Australian, Les Murray, has said he is using more rhyme now, as indeed he is. So out of the closet with you, secret rhymers, and remember, such obviously serious poets as Hopkins and Dylan Thomas rhymed (trisyllabically too) all the time, though it is true a lot of it was internal. What is internal rhyme? I will come to that.

A long series of full masculine rhymes can have a rather thumping effect. That may be the effect you want. Vachel Lindsay tramped round the West when it was still wild, reading his ballads out in saloons. This is from 'Simon Legree'. The wicked slaver from 'Uncle Tom's Cabin' has died and checked into Hell, which strikes him very favourably:

> I see that you have much to eat –
> A red ham-bone is surely sweet.
> I see that you have lion's feet;
> I see your frame is fat and fine,
> I see you drink your poison wine –
> Blood and burning turpentine.

I love that and I'm sure it went down well with the cowboys. But there *are* ways of softening that thump. Les Murray's 'The Sleepout' begins:

> Childhood sleeps in a verandah room
> In an iron bed close to the wall
> where the winter over the railing
> swelled the blind on its timber boom
>
> and splinters picked lint off warm linen
> and the stars were out over the hill;
> and one wall of the room was forest
> and all things in there were to come.

There are the full masculine rhymes 'room/boom' and then there is 'come' which is not quite a rhyme. There is the consonance 'wall/hill' and the three feminine endings 'railing/linen/forest'. The last word of the last line of the poem is 'moon' which nearly (but not quite) rhymes with 'room' at the beginning. Then there are the repetitions of 'wall' and 'room' and other words that rhyme or chime internally. Many other modern poets, Heaney notably, prefer to rhyme, or at least to chime, in these ways.

Some definitions

Actually these are not definitions, which seem to get impossibly complicated, just examples. And the terminology sometimes differs. Pararhyme can be called 'slant rhyme', for instance. Then there is the word 'chime' which seems to cover any similarity of sound which isn't a full rhyme. And remember – never stop remembering – that poetry is not a matter of definitions and rules and right or wrong. Poets, though often timid souls in the big, bad world, are by nature rule-breakers when the Muse is speaking to them. They bend and stretch what they are given, they make the language do new things. Which is surely as it should be. Now the examples:

Types of rhyme

1. Full rhyme	great/mate/contemplate
2. Rime riche or perfect rhyme	**great/great/grate**
3. Eye rhyme	great/sweat/feat
4. Pararhyme	great/groat/greet
5. Assonance (of vowels)	great/fail/displayed
6. Consonance (of consonants)	great/coat/repeat

There is perhaps one more kind of rhyme which, as far as I know, has no technical name – I mean the ludicrous:

> Come all you lord of ladies in**tellectual**
> Inform us truly, have they not **henpecked you all**

You will find plenty more of these scattered through 'Don Juan', the long, uneven masterpiece which Byron claimed he wrote in part while he was shaving (presumably being shaved) and which I confess I have never read right through. Browning liked this sort of thing too. In 'The Pied Piper of Hamelin' he rhymed psaltery/drysaltery, obese/robe ease and even promise/from mice. My all-time favourite is by Norman Levy:

> I blushed up to the hat o' me
> To see that girl's anatomy

In centuries before the Modern movement, poets did not generally use the near-rhymes 4–6; they seem to have been regarded as cheating – though eye-rhymes (love/move), which are a kind of consonance plus, and rime riche (slay/sleigh or even slay/slay) were OK. Some near-rhyme examples turn out not to be proper examples at all, like this one from Alexander Pope (Great Anna is Queen Anne and the three realms England, Scotland and Ireland):

> Hear thou, Great Anna, whom three realms obey,
> Doth sometimes counsel take – and sometimes tea.

In the 18th century 'tea' was pronounced 'tay', at least by the smart set – that is part of the joke. Pope could also rhyme **besieged/obliged** (obleeged) and Shakespeare's **swan/can** was a full rhyme.

The old poets allowed themselves all sorts of inversions of the natural word-order for the sake of rhyme or metre, which we would probably prefer not to use. Keats, for instance, speaks of 'faery lands forlorn' partly because he needs a rhyme for 'corn'. And earlier in the same Ode, he wishes he might be like the Nightingale:

> And with thee fade away into the forest dim:

I wouldn't change a word of this, but what was good for Keats then may not suit us now. English must be kept up, even if that doesn't make it any easier.

MacNeice's run-on over the rhyme has a very long history. This is the first stanza of Sir Thomas Wyatt's most famous poem, written in the time of Henry the Eighth. I have used a forward slash (/) to show where I suppose a sensitive reader would pause. According to me, this happens only twice at line-ends (lines 2 and 3); all the others are enjambed.

> They flee from me/ that sometime did me seek
> With naked foot,/ stalking in my chamber,/
> I have seen them, /gentle, tame, and meek,/
> That now are wild,/ and do not remember
> That sometime/ they put themselves in danger
> To take bread at my hand,/ and now they range
> Busily seeking,/ with a continual change.

Some of these rhymes look rather modern; chamber/remember/danger – all feminine, and there is a chime (danger/range). Wyatt is a poet whose stock went up in the first half of the 20th century – he has a Modernist feel.

Rhymes that are not rhymes have an effect all their own. Look at MacNeice again, in his rightly celebrated 'Bagpipe Music'.

> It's no go the merrygoround, it's no go the **rickshaw**,
> All we want is a limousine and a ticket for the **peepshow**,
> Their knickers are made of crepe-de-chine, their shoes are made of
>   **python**,
> Their halls are lined with tiger rugs and their walls with heads of
>   **bison**.

This is one of the poems that first made me want to be a poet and has been much parodied, usually with full rhymes, either because it is easier or because the parodist hasn't noticed. None of MacNeice's rhymes are full. Check the poem if you don't believe me. Of course he is being funny. But Wilfred Owen, using masculine rhymes where MacNeice sticks to feminine ones, is not:

> My soul looks down from a vague height, with **death**,
> As unremembering how I rose or **why**,
> And saw a sad land, wet with sweats of **dearth**,
> Gray, cratered like the moon with hollow **woe**,
> And pitted with great pocks, and scabs of **plagues**.
> Across its beard, that horror of harsh **wire**,
> There moved thin caterpillars, slowly **uncoiled**,
> It seemed they pushed themselves to be as **plugs**
> Of ditches, where they writhed and shrivelled, **killed**.

It is actually quite difficult to write poems with off-rhymes like this, and there is no rhyming dictionary to help you.

Exercise 21: Off-rhymes

Write a poem of at least ten lines where every line rhymes with at least one other but where none of the rhymes are full ones. What counts as a rhyme? Look at the examples above. I have put into heavy type the parts of the words that match, as it were, and included MacNeice's next two sets of rhymes:

MacNeice

rickshaw/peepshow
python/bison
sofa/poker
whiskey/fifty

Owen

why/woe/wire
death/dearth
plagues/plugs
coiled/killed

Here is a (far from exhaustive) list of words which have no full rhymes in English. Use some/most/all of them in your poem. Of course, you do not have to use my suggested near-rhymes.

breadth, circle, desert, monarch, month, orange, silver, virtue, wisdom

Possible near-rhymes would be:

breath, ankle, effort, panic, munch, carver, shoe, random

Internal rhyme

There is no rule that says rhymes have to come at the end of a line; those that do not are called *internal rhymes*. Dylan Thomas uses them to good effect in 'Under Milk Wood' and Gerard Manley Hopkins uses them all the time:

How to keep – is there any any, is there none such, nowhere known
 some, bow or brooch or braid or **brace**, **lace**, **latch** or **catch** or key to keep
Back beauty, keep it beauty, beauty, beauty ... from vanishing away

There are, in the same long line, such pairings as **nowhere/known**, **bow/brooch** and **key/keep** which are not strictly rhymes (they are assonance) but which have much the same effect. And there is the effect of all those initial sounds k, **b** and l, which we call alliteration.

Alliteration

> Guinness is good for you
> Electro**lux** brings **lux**ury to life
> You can be sure of **Sh**ell

The advertising industry loves alliteration. It loves rhyme as well but it loves alliteration more – meaning the repetition usually of a consonantal sound, often, but not always, an initial consonantal sound as in the first and third examples. There is a richer alliteration in the second example, the repetition of the consonant/vowel/consonant cluster **lux**. You can alliterate on vowels also, as Gavin Ewart does in his 'A Possible Line of John Clare':

> A little tittlemouse goes twiddling by

Shakespeare alliterated as naturally as he breathed:

> After life's fitful fever he sleeps well.

says Macbeth of Duncan. Othello speaks of his revenge as:

> Like to the **P**ontick sea,
> Whose icy **c**urrent and **c**ompulsive **c**ourse
> Ne'er feels retiring e**bb**, **b**ut **k**eeps due on
> To the **P**ro**p**ontic and the Helles**p**ont

Victorians were particularly fond of it. Tennyson:

> **S**weet is every **s**ound,
> **S**weeter thy voice, but every **s**ound is **s**weet;
> **M**yriads of rivulets hurrying thro' the lawn,
> The **m**oan of doves in i**mm**emorial elms,
> And **m**ur**m**urings of innu**m**erable bees.

Hopkins alliterated practically anywhere – look at the internally rhyming excerpt above. Swinburne couldn't resist it:

> Thou hast conquered, O pale Galilean; the world has grown grey from thy breath;
> Thou hast drunken of things Lethean, and fed on the fullness of death.

There is a touch of intellectual snobbery about alliteration nowadays; you feel some poets are so subtle they would never employ anything so obvious. But three of Eliot's most celebrated lines alliterate famously:

> April is the cruellest month, breeding
> Lilacs out of the dead land, mixing
> Memory and desire ...

Larkin does not disdain it in the first stanza of 'The Explosion':

> On the day of the explosion
> Shadows pointed towards the pithead:
> In the sun the slagheap slept.

Nor (of course) does Dylan Thomas, nor does Charles Causley at the opening of 'Guy Fawkes' Day':

> I am the caught, the cooked, the candled man
> With flames for fingers and whose thin eyes fountain,

But we all of us alliterate, just as I said Shakespeare did, as naturally as breathing. Look at these idioms/clichés:

> Through thick and thin
> In weal and woe
> With kith and kin
> We boldly go
> Till safe and sound
> From the bitter blast
> We go to ground
> At long, long last.

Alliterative metre

Old English verse did not rhyme; it alliterated according to a strict pattern. As *The Princeton Handbook of Poetic Terms* has it:

> The long line ... is divided into two metrically independent verses by a pause, and the verse pairs are linked by the alliteration of one or two stressed syllables in the first verse with the first stressed syllable in the second verse.

Anglo-Saxons liked alliterative riddles. Here is a modern alliterative riddle.

Internet, intercom	inter-relational
Syndicate, synergy	systems analysis,
Online, ongoing,	on message, on-target,
Download, downsizing and	down in the mouth

UA Fanthorpe's riddle is a little freer with the alliterative rule, but the general idea is still there.

A door	but not a door
In homes	but not for humans
I have no hole	for a key, nor a handle,
Those who flash through me	having no fingers.
I am way out	and way in
For the night-watchers,	the long-whiskered.

The solution? I'll give you a clue – the long-whiskered are not mice, quite the contrary really.

Exercise 22: Riddle-me-ree
Invent an alliterative riddle of your own. Stick to the four-beat alliterative line broken into two parts:

Write me a rhymeless	riddle-me-ree.
Lock it with letters,	seal it with learning.

Answers to riddles
Mine is a modern office and Fanthorpe's a cat-door. Peter Reading is a fine riddler. His anwers tend to be things like death and strait-jackets, which would please those Anglo-Saxons.

12. Some Verse Forms

The simplest rhyming verse is the couplet.

> Oranges and lemons
> Say the bells of Saint Clements.
> I owe you five farthings
> Say the bells of Saint Martins.
> When will you pay me
> Say the bells of Old Bailey ...

These six lines can be represented using the letters of the alphabet as **aabbcc**. It is a very old form. A 12th century poem called 'The Owl and the Nightingale', in which the two birds debate which is the better singer, is written in tetrameter rhyming couplets. Many of Chaucer's 'Canterbury Tales' (14th century) are in pentameters.

> A knyght ther was, and that a worthy man,
> That fro the tyme that he first bigan
> To riden out, he lov**ed** chivalrie,
> Trouthe and honour, fredom and curtesie.

You must pronounce the letters in heavy type as if they were syllables. Rechristened the heroic couplet, this was the usual vehicle for poetry in the Neo-Classical Age from 1660 to around 1780. Doctor Johnson claimed he could compose 50 verses (that's 100 lines) in his head. Pope's 'Epistle to Miss Blount, on her leaving the Town' is typical in everything except its great skill:

> **She went,** to plain work, and to purling brooks,
> Old fashioned halls, dull aunts, and croaking rooks,
> **She went** from Op'ra, park, assembly, play,
> **To** morning walks and prayers three times a day;
> **To** pass her time 'twixt reading and Bohea,   [a kind of tea]
> **To** muse and spill her solitary Tea,   [pronounced 'tay']

> Or o'er cold coffee trifle with the spoon,
> **Count** the slow clock, and **dine** exact at noon;
> **Divert** her eyes with pictures in the fire,
> **Hum** half a tune, **tell** stories to the squire;
> Up to her godly garret after seven,
> There starve and pray, for that's the way to heaven.

The lines are metrically very regular. By writing 'op'ra', ''twixt' and 'o'er', Pope makes sure that we will read each as ten syllables exactly (except the concluding couplet with its feminine rhymes) and every line is end-stopped. What prevents it from fragmenting into a necklace of little two-line poems is the rhetorical structure (highlighted in heavy type) of its single long sentence.

A couplet can be short:

> A pint of beer
> Will bring good cheer;
> A pint of wine
> Is mighty fine;
> But a pint of gin
> Will do you in.

Or long:

> As I in hoary winter's night stood shivering in the snow,
> Surprised I was with sudden heat which made my heart to glow;
> And lifting up a fearful eye to view what fire was near,
> A pretty babe all burning bright did in the air appear;

But any line longer than five stresses tends to break in two. Many seven-stress couplets – the example is from the Elizabethan poet Robert Southwell's 'The Burning Babe' – could be written out in quatrains of alternate four and three stresses. We can write this **abcb** which shows that the second and fourth lines (the two **b**s) rhyme and the first and third (**a** and **c**) do not:

> As I in hoary winter's night
>   Stood shivering in the snow
> Surprised I was with sudden heat
>   Which made my heart to glow;

This is the ballad stanza – most of the old ballads were written in it.

There lived a wife in Usher's Well,
    And a wealthy wife was she;
She had three stout and stalwart sons
    And she sent them o'er the sea ...

Quatrains

Romantic poets like Keats, Scott and Coleridge were inspired by ballads:

And now there came both mist and snow,
    And it grew wondrous cold:
And ice, mast high, came floating by,
    As green as emerald.

Those internal rhymes in line 3 are found in ballads too.

The cock doth craw, the day doth daw,
    The channerin worm doth chide.

If you make the first and third lines of the stanza rhyme also (**abab**) you have a hymn meter known as short, or common, measure.

God moves in a mysterious way,
    His wonders to perform:
He plants his footsteps in the sea
    And rides upon the storm.

You can shorten it still further, dispensing with the second set of rhymes:

Jerusalem the golden
    With milk and honey blest,
Beneath thy contemplation
    Sink heart and voice oppressed.

Four stresses throughout, and all rhymes restored, gives you long measure:

When I survey the wondrous cross
On which the Prince of Glory died,
My richest gain I count but loss,
And pour contempt on all my pride.

These verses are by William Cowper, John Mason Neale and Isaac Watts respectively. Modern poets – Betjeman, Eliot, Auden – have tended to use quatrains for comic or satiric purposes, and many of Emily Dickinson's extraordinary effects arise out of the tension between simple form and sophisticated content:

> My life closed twice before its close –
> It yet remains to see
> If Immortality unveil
> A third event for me.

or:

> My Life had stood – a Loaded Gun –
> In corners – till a Day
> The Owner passed – identified –
> And carried Me away –

or:

> But never met this fellow
> Attended or alone
> Without a tighter breathing
> And zero at the bone.

Long measure was a favourite of metaphysical poets. This is from Donne's 'A Valediction: Forbidding Mourning':

> Dull sublunary lovers love
>   (Whose soul is sense) cannot admit
> Absence, because it doth remove
>   Those things which elemented it,
>
> But we by a love so much refin'd,
>   That our selves know not what it is,
> Inter-assured of the mind,
>   Care lesse, eyes, lips, and hands to miss.

If you lengthen the lines to pentameter you get the quatrain of Thomas Gray's 'Elegy in a Country Churchyard', often known as the elegiac stanza:

There scatter'd oft, the earliest of the Year,
By hands unseen, are show'rs of Violets found;
The Red-breast loves to build and warble there,
And little footsteps lightly print the ground.

Two couplets together makes a quatrain rhyming **aabb** (Southwell above). A certain metrical 'oh that'll do!' quality may give such a quatrain a careless, devil-may-care swing, as in Larkin's 'Money', or this:

Talk to me, Thoth, it's good to talk,
My wordhoard Lord, with the head of a Stork,
With the soul of a dog and a Monkey's bum.
Talk to me, Thoth, till your kingdom come.

Housman's 'Oh who is that young sinner' has a recurring refrain for the last line; Marvell's 'Horatian Ode' (*see* Chapter 5) employs couplets of varying length. You need somehow to escape the effect of heroic or tetrameter couplets yoked together for no good reason.

Tennyson's 'In Memoriam' uses the rhyme scheme **abba**:

The hills are shadows, and they flow
    From form to form, and nothing stands;
    They melt like mists, the solid lands,
Like clouds they shape themselves and go.

A couplet encloses another couplet; put two of these together (as you do in the octet of a Petrarchan sonnet) and you get a shifting pattern of enclosures: **abbaabba** could be **(abba)(abba)** or **ab(baab)ba** or even chinese boxes **a[bb(aa)bb]a**. Edward Fitzgerald's 'The Rubaiyat of Omar Khayyam' rhymes **aaba**, leaving the third line unrhymed and unresolved:

Ah, Moon of my Delight who know'st no wane,
The Moon of Heav'n is rising once again:
How oft hereafter rising shall she look
Through this same Garden after me – in vain.

It is as if there is a very long line indeed after the intitial couplet; dying away until caught up just in time by the final rhyme. And you can substitute chimes for rhymes if you don't want that affirmative snap at the line end:

Some nights you could hear the whole house breathing
And a tap-tapping at the wainscot
That was rats that was fat black rats
Scratching and sniffing and snuffling for a way in

Triplets

When the Restoration Poet Laureate, John Dryden, writes a couplet:

'Twas in a grove of spreading Pines he stray'd;
The Winds within the quiv'ring Branches play'd

and adds a third rhyming line:

And Dancing Trees a mournful Musick made

he has a triplet, which he uses to vary his couplets, often
lengthening the last line by a foot. Whole poems can be written in
triplets, like this celebrated short lyric by Robert Herrick:

Whenas in silks my Julia goes,
Then, then (methinks) how sweetly flows
The liquefaction of her clothes.

Next, when I cast mine eyes and see
That brave vibration each way free,
Oh, how that glittering taketh me.

Such stanzas will hardly bear sustained argument – the insistent
rhymes tend to mark every stanza off as a separate unit – but they
work well in light verse. Lewis Carroll's 'The Three Voices' is a
parody (of Tennyson) with a life of its own:

Dead calm succeeded to the fuss,
As when the loaded omnibus
Has reached the railway terminus:

When, for the tumult of the street,
Is heard the engine's stifled beat,
The velvet tread of porter's feet.

The interlocking rhymes of Dante's *terza rima* (aba bcb . . .) are
tricky to manage, but the stanzas (also called tercets) do run on well,
as you can see in this excerpt from Shelley's 'The Triumph of Life':

114

... The grove

Grew dense with shadows to its inmost covers,
The earth was grey with phantoms, and the air
Was peopled with dim forms, as when there hovers

A flock of vampire bats before the glare
Of the tropic sun, bringing, ere evening,
Strange nights upon some Indian Isle: – thus were

Phantoms diffused around; and some did fling
Shadows of shadows, yet unlike themselves,
Behind them, some, like eaglets on the wing,

Were lost in the white day;

Modern poets often rhyme their triplets irregularly or dispense with
rhyme altogether. Wallace Stevens' 'Sea Surface with Clouds' takes
the first option; his 'Notes Towards a Supreme Fiction' the second.

Long and short lines

The 17th century liked them – Donne and Herbert particularly – but
perhaps the king of the long and short line poem is Thomas Hardy.

'Who's in the next room? – who?
    A figure wan
With a message to one in there of something due?
    Shall I know him anon?'
'Yea he; and he brought such; and you'll know him anon.

Variable line length, repetition and enjambment combine to play
down the effect of the rhyme so that you get a kind of counter-
point between the formal structure and the meaning. Betjeman
and Larkin, among others, learned much from Hardy.

Longer stanzas

If you add a rhyming line after line 3 of the ballad stanza you get
a pleasant **abccb** stanza (a form of *quinzaine*) that Coleridge was
very fond of (*see* Chapter 1). Two lines added to a quatrain makes
a *sixaine*:

The Walrus and the Carpenter
Were walking close at hand:
They wept like anything to see
Such quantities of sand:
'If all this could be cleared away,'
They said, 'It would be grand.'

Wilde's 'The Ballad of Reading Gaol' uses the same stanza. Alternatively, you can add a closing couplet, as Ben Jonson does:

Queen and huntress, chaste and fair,
Now the sun is laid to sleep,
Seated in thy silver chair,
State in wonted manner keep:
Hesperus entreats thy light,
Goddess excellently bright.

If, in the pentameter version of this stanza, you add a rhyming line after line 4, then you will have the septaine known as the *rhyme royal* stanza Chaucer used in his long poem 'Troilus and Criseyde':

All things that love the sun are out of doors;
Thy sky rejoices in the morning's birth;
The grass is bright with rain-drops; on the moors
The hare is running races in her mirth;
And with her feet she from the plashy earth
Raises a mist; which, glittering in the sun,
Runs with her all the way, wherever she doth run.

That stanza is not Chaucer, but Wordsworth ('Resolution and Independence'). He varies the pattern with an Alexandrine – six-stress – line at the end. Graves and Auden have written in this stanza.

Add a couplet to long measure and you have *ottava rima*, a favourite vehicle of Byron. This is from 'A Vision of Judgement' (Byron suggested in the previous stanza that eternal punishment is an unchristian notion):

I know this is unpopular; I know
    'Tis blasphemous. I know one may be damned
For hoping no one else may e'er be so;
    I know my catechism; I know we're crammed
With the best doctrines till we quite o'erflow;

I know that all save England's church have shammed,
And that the other twice two hundred churches
And synagogues have made a *damned* bad purchase.

Keats, Shelley, Yeats and James Fenton (his Vietnam poem 'In a Notebook') have all used this stanza.

Two interlocking stanzas of long measure, using only three rhymes and a final Alexandrine that rhymes with the line before it, give us the *Spenserian* stanza. This was used by Spenser for 'The Faerie Queen' (all 36,000 lines of it), Byron ('Childe Harold'), Keats ('The Eve of Saint Agnes'), Shelley ('Adonais') and Tennyson ('The Lotos Eaters'). It rhymes **ababbcbcc**. This is Keats:

She danced along with vague, regardless eyes,
Anxious her lips, her breathing quick and short;
The hallowed hour was near at hand: she sighs
Amid the timbrels, and the thronged resort
Of whisperers in anger, or in sport;
'Mid looks of love, defiance, hate, and scorn,
Hoodwinked with faery fancy; all amort,
Save to St Agnes and her lambs unshorn,
And all the bliss to be before tomorrow morn.

Few modern poets (except me) use this stanza, though Robert Lowell's 'Christmas Eve Under Hooker's Statue' is quite close. Perhaps it seems too languid – go-getters that we are.

Where does it say that you can't use your own stanza? Francis Thompson did in his celebrated 'At Lord's':

It is little I repair to the matches of the Southron folk,
    Though my own red roses there may blow;
It is little I repair to the matches of the Southron folk,
    Though the red rose crest their caps, I know.
For the field is full of shades as I reach the shadowy coast,
And a ghostly batsman plays to the bowling of a ghost,
And I look through my tears on a soundless, clapping host
    As the run-stealers flicker to and fro,
    To and fro:
O my Hornby and my Barlow long ago!

Look at the rhythmic shift in the second and fourth lines. Other noted stanzaic innovators are Hardy (of course), Larkin, Betjeman, Glyn Maxwell and Sophie Hannah.

Exercise 23: Couplet tennis

A very simple game, and a very old one too. You need another poet. Make up a line in a particular metre and pass it to your partner/opponent. I have taken this one at random from *The New Oxford Book of Victorian Verse*:

> My father was a scholar and knew Greek

Your partner adds a rhyming line to make a couplet:

> My mother fancied dancing cheek to **cheek**

And then another that follows on but does *not* rhyme with the preceding two:

> They were not suited. News of the divorce

Your partner passes it back and you add two more lines, one rhyming with what precedes it and one not:

> Was sent to me by semaphore and **morse**
> While I was mountain climbing in Peru

Back again:

> With Biffy, Clumps and Pongo, the old **crew**
> I used to mess about with back at College

And so on, until boredom sets in or you can't find a good rhyme ('college' has only one as far as I know). Advanced learners can try more complex forms than the simple couplet.

13. Sonnets

You could make an anthology of English poetry using nothing but sonnets and the only century under-represented would be the 18th – Dryden, Pope and Johnson wrote no sonnets that I know of.

Who has written sonnets?
Wyatt, Sidney, Spenser, Shakespeare, Milton, Wordsworth, Coleridge, Shelley, Keats, Elizabeth Barrett, Hopkins, Dante Gabriel Rossetti, Christina Rossetti, Rupert Brooke, Wilfred Owen, Yeats, Auden, Dylan Thomas, Robert Garioch, Larkin, Heaney, Edwin Morgan, Les Murray, Sophie Hannah, Wendy Cope, Simon Armitage – and most of the poets that I like.

We have already seen that modern poets tend to use different kinds of near-rhyme as often as full rhymes, not from lack of skill but for preference. These, for instance, are the rhyme-words of Simon Armitage's 'Poem':

drive/side/night/lied
wage/saved/made/face
nurse/church/worse/purse/back/that

Armitage uses assonance to bind his quatrains together with occasional full rhyme (side/lied, nurse/worse/purse). However, I suggest that, if you are not practised in sonnet writing, you keep fairly to the traditional form until you have managed to write half a dozen (all right – three). It is easier to stick to the rules than to break them: until you are a practised poet, you will not know which ways of breaking the rules are interesting, and which merely crass. In the words of Jorge Luis Borges:

> ... the difference between, let's say, a sonnet by Keats and a page of free verse by Whitman, lies in the fact that, in the case of the sonnet the structure is obvious – and so it is easier to do – while if you try

to write something like 'Children of Adam' or 'Song of Myself' you have to invent your own structure. Without structure the poem would be shapeless, and I don't think it can afford to be that.

Before we go any further we had better decide exactly what a sonnet is. In the 16th and 17th centuries the word 'sonnet' was used for any short lyric. But our definition is tighter. Here is a checklist:

A sonnet:
- is **14 lines** (but *see* Meredith and Hopkins below)
- of **iambic pentameter** (but *see* Hopkins below)
- **rhyming** according to one of a number of traditional rhyme-schemes
- and split into **two parts**: 8 lines (the **octet**) and 6 lines (the **sestet**).

That last is true of many sonnets, but not all, as we shall see.

The Petrarchan (or Italian) sonnet

This is named after the Italian poet Petrarch and rhymes according to this pattern: **abbaabba cdecde** (or **cdcdcd** or any other combination or two or three rhyme words that avoids a couplet at the end).

The following example by Milton shows the shape of a Petrarchan sonnet – eight lines then the 'turn' and six more: argument and development, observation and conclusion, statement and counter-statement. In the octet Milton suggests – prudentially, for he was politically very active and had many enemies – that his status as a poet should give him political amnesty at all times. In the sestet he develops this argument by suggesting two historical parallels: that Alexander the Great (the Emathian conqueror) gave protection to the house of the poet Pindar; and that the Spartan general Lysander did the same for the dramatist Euripides at the end of the Peloponnesian War. ('Colonel' should be pronounced with three syllables.)

> Captain or Colonel or Knight in **Arms**
> Whose chance on these defenceless doors may **seize**,
> If deeds of honour did thee ever **please**,
> Guard them, and him within protect from **harms**,
> He can requite thee, for he knows the **charms**
> That call Fame on such gentle acts as **these**,
> And he can spread thy name o'er Lands and **Seas**,
> Whatever clime the Sun's bright circle **warms**.

> Lift not thy spear against the Muse's **Bower**,
> The great Emathian Conqueror bid **spare**
> The house of Pindarus, when Temple and **Tower**
> Went to the ground: and the repeated **air**
> Of sad Electra's Poet had the **power**
> To save th'Athenian walls from ruin **bare.**

A problem can be just finding enough good rhymes for the octet and then, when you do, not allowing them to overwhelm the poem. Milton allows the eye-rhyme **warms** (but was it an eye-rhyme to him?) and much inversion of the natural word order; in line 2 he writes 'chance on these defenceless doors may seize' instead of 'chance may seize on these defenceless doors'. You find similar inversions in lines 3, 4 and 8. But Milton uses inversion in 'Paradise Lost' where he has no problem with rhymes; he does it partly because he wants his English to sound like Latin, which commonly puts verbs at the ends of sentences and adjectives after their nouns. But he has other reasons: the euphonious last line of the sonnet

> To save th'Athenian walls from ruin bare

would be less effective, surely, if it ended 'bare ruin', even if there were no rhymes to consider. And what would rhyme with 'ruin' – 'bruin', 'threw in', 'doin' pronounced aristocratically? Milton might not have found the search for rhymes a problem. He makes a joke (yes, Milton does make jokes) about it, beginning a sonnet this way:

> A book was writ of late called Tetrachordon;

(his own book actually) and rhymes with 'pored on', 'word on' and 'Gordon' (a joke about barbarous Scots names). Another sonnet begins with a scatter of plosive consonants:

> I **d**id **b**ut **p**rompt: the age **to q**uit their **cl**ogs:

This, amusingly (to my mind), suggests various cacophonous animals (**dogs, frogs, hogs**) which duly turn up as rhyme words.

One of the best, certainly the most remarkable formally, of all English Petrarchan sonnets is Hopkins' 'The Windhover', which show just how far you can go with enjambment (the sense running on over the rhyme into the next line). Hopkins wrote it in what he called 'sprung' rhythm, allowing for many more unstressed syllables. His syllable count for a line (16 in line 3, 15 in lines 2, 4 and 6) might be a record for a pentameter sonnet, if he didn't break it himself in 'Duns Scotus's Oxford' and (repeatedly) in 'Spelt From Sibyl's Leaves'. With Hopkins' help, I have marked stresses in heavy type for the long lines.

> I caught this morning morning's minion, king-
>> dom of **daylight's dauphin**, dapple-**dawn**-drawn **Falcon**, in his **riding**
>> Of the **rolling** level **underneath** him **steady air**, and **striding**
> **High** there, how he **rung** upon the **rein** of a **wimpling wing**
> In his ecstasy! Then off, off forth on a swing,
>> As a **skate's** heel sweeps **smooth** on a **bow**-bend: the **hurl** and **gliding**
>> Rebuffed the big wind. My heart in hiding
> Stirred for a bird – the achieve of, the mastery of the thing!
>
> Brute beauty and valour and act, oh, air, pride, plume, here
>> Buckle! AND the fire that breaks from thee then, a billion
> Times told lovelier, more dangerous, O my chevalier!
>
>> No wonder of it: sheer plod makes plough down sillion
> Shine, and blue-bleak embers, ah my dear,
>> Fall, gall themselves, and gash gold-vermilion.

A 'sillion' is a furrow, as you might have guessed. I hope, and believe, that Hopkins picked the word up locally rather than found it in a dictionary.

The Shakespearian (or English) sonnet

This was not invented by Shakespeare, but nearly all of his sonnets are written in its form: **ababcdcdefefgg**. There are two things to note about this: first, that such sonnets are much easier to write because you do not have to cast around for rhymes; and second, that the division signalled by the rhymes, is 4, 4, 4, 2 rather than 8, 6. You can see this clearly in Sonnet 30:

> **When** to the session of sweet silent thought
> I summon up remembrance of things past,
> I sigh the lack of many a thing I sought,
> And with old woes new wail my dear time's waste:
> **Then** can I drown an eye, unused to flow,
> For precious friends hid in death's dateless night,
> And weep afresh love's long since cancelled woe,

And moan th'expense of many a vanished sight.
Then can I grieve at grievances foregone,
And heavily from woe to woe tell o'er
The sad account of fore-bemoaned moan,
Which I new pay as if not paid before.
  But if the while I think on thee, dear friend,
  All losses are restored and sorrows end.

When (1) I think of the past, **then** (2) I feel a sense of loss and **then** (3) that makes me feel sad afresh **but** (4) the thought of you makes up for it. The final couplet ought to clinch the argument, but I am not sure that it does – Shakespeare's couplets can be perfunctory; one tends not to believe them.

The Spenserian sonnet, invented (perhaps) by Shakespeare's contemporary Edmund Spenser, uses an interlocking rhyme scheme **ababbcbccdcdee**, reminiscent of the stanza he invented for 'The Faerie Queene' – that long (36,000 lines) unfinished epic every poet ought to read . . . once. The division is 12/2 rather than 8/6.

Both Keats and Shelley took up the idea of interlocking rhyme, though not the Spenserian form. Shelley's 'Ozymandias' and his 'Ode to the West Wind' (actually a sequence of five sonnets, though it is easy not to notice this and I am indebted to John Fuller for pointing it out) both use an interlocking structure. My personal favourite, 'England in 1819', uses just four rhymes (**ababababcdcdccdd**) and the repetition thuds like a hammer. Shelley, far from the 'ineffectual angel' of tradition, was splendid at contemptuous political invective. You can't recite this poem without spitting with hatred:

An old, mad, blind, despised and dying king, –
Princes, the dregs of their dull race, who flow
Through public scorn, – mud from a muddy spring,
Rulers who neither see, nor feel, nor know,
But leech-like to their fainting country cling.
Till they drop, blind in blood, without a blow, –
A people starved and stabbed in the untilled field, –
An army, which liberticide and prey
Makes as a two-edged sword to all who wield, –
Golden and sanguine laws which tempt and slay;
Religion Christless, Godless – a book sealed:
A Senate, – Time's worst statute unrepealed, –
Are graves, from which a glorious Phantom may
Burst, to illumine our tempestuous day.

The 12/2 division is clear: the first 12 lines enumerate the bad, old things – king, princes, people in slavery, army, religion, senate – and the last two hold out the hope that change may come, through revolution presumably.

Variations

Hopkins writes 'curtal' sonnets – that is curtailed sonnets of 10½ lines, split 6/4½. Meredith's 'Modern Love' is a series of 'sonnets' of 16 lines divided into four **abba** stanzas, and Tony Harrison writes 16-liners also (rhyming **abab**). Auden shortens one sonnet drastically in the sestet and divides another 3/3/3/3/2 (like Shelley in 'Ode to the West Wind'). Larkin adds an extra last line ('Arrivals, Departures'). Gavin Ewart (and others) write sonnets that do not rhyme at all. I have written a sonnet on two rhymes only (**ababab...**); Kit Wright has (nearly) written one, 'A Clubman's Ozymandias', on one.

Two modern sonnets

In 'The Forge', Seamus Heaney covers his tracks so well in at least three ways that the careless reader might not realise he was writing a sonnet at all.

1. The lines are mostly metric variations: only lines 3, 6, 9 and 11 are straight iambics; line 8, on my count, has only three stresses; lines 12/13 are primarily trochaic and dactylic.

2. The octet continues for an extra line until the turn at 'music'.

3. His rhyme scheme (**abbacddcefcfef**) is unusual, and disguised with some cunning. He juxtaposes masculine and feminine rhymes (rusting/ring, centre/square/clatter, music/flick, nose/rows/bellows); there are internal rhymes (new/shoe, somewhere/centre, traffic/flick) and chimes (hammered anvil, unpredictable/fantail, horned as a unicorn) – all combining to play down the bravura, slightly show-off effect neat end-rhymes tend to have.

The effect he does get is slow, ruminative, something that looks back to the old alliterative verse tradition (there is plenty of alliteration – just look), highly wrought yet at the same time free, or at least giving the *illusion* of freedom.

The Forge

All I know is a door into the dark,
Outside, old axles and iron hoops rusting;
Inside, the hammered anvil's short-pitched ring,
The unpredictable fantail of sparks
Or hiss when a new shoe toughens in water.
The anvil must be somewhere in the centre,
Horned as a unicorn, at one end square,
Set there, immoveable, an altar
Where he expends himself in shape and music.
Sometimes, leather-aproned, hairs in his nose,
He leans out on the jamb, recalls a clatter
Of hooves where traffic is flashing in rows;
Then grunts and goes in with a slam and flick
To beat real iron out, to work the bellows.

Who would not wish to write half as well as this? But there is no limit to the variations you *can* invent and poets have not yet got bored with the form (will they ever be?). Peter Howard's 'A Simple and Uncomplicated Sonnet, in Which the Poet Remarks on the Diversity in Expectation and Aspiration among Human Kind', takes a love affair with the dictionary about as far as it will go.

Enthusiastic echolalia
Eclectic, euphuistic Icarus
Conveys on wings to where the angels are
And panegyrics disingenuous.
His lucubrations are all fantasy,
Wherein each continent would be his own:
Discovers isochronous with the sea,
The ineluctable brachistochrone.
Vituperation by the troglodyte
Will not triumphant celebration dull;
To such a hedonistic sybarite
Ephemera are also palpable.
    He captures one encomiastic kiss:
    His transient epeirogenesis.

My computer's thesaurus gives up on this so I shall append the glossary Howard sent me.

echolalia: compulsive or senseless repetition of words heard
eclectic: drawing from a number of sources

euphuistic: (of speech) elaborate or high-flown
Icarus: guy who flew too near the sun, so his wings fell off
panegyrics: eulogies
idisingenous: not frank – I mean insincere
lucubrations: night-time study
isochronous: at the same time as
ineluctable: unavoidable
brachistochrone: curve along which a particle acted on by a force passes
   in the shortest time from one point to another
vituperation: abusive verbal attack – I mean criticism
troglodyte: cave-dweller, but I mean glum, unwelcome, critic type of person
hedonistioc: living for the day
sybarite: person devoted to luxury
ephemera: things that don't last
encomiastic: bestowing praise
epeirogenesis: the formation of continents – I mean earth-moving

Sonnets are obsessional. The American Merrill Moore wrote *more than 100,000* and had a building constructed behind his house entirely filled with steel filing cabinets to keep them in.

Exercise 24: Seven sonnet variations

1. The same Peter Howard has written 'A Useful Sonnet' entirely made up of household tips such as 'Clean varnished floors by rubbing with cold tea' and 'An old crisp packet makes a useful condom' (don't try that one). Compose a sonnet of your own made up of sayings, clichés, proverbs. You should (I think) mix up real proverbs, etc. with imaginary ones like Wendy Cope's 'fine words won't turn the icing pink'. It is probably simpler if you stick, more or less, to the pattern of one per line.

2. Write a sonnet with a given set of rhyme words. This is a favourite of *The Spectator*'s literary competitions set by Jaspistos (the poet James Michie). Try one of these. The rhyme words belong to sonnets by Wordsworth, Sophie Hannah and Les Murray respectively. Probably the Murray is the hardest – how are you going to get 'insufflation' in? You could cheat, I suppose and use another 'ation' word.

❏ fee/worth/birth/liberty/free/violate/mate/sea/fade/decay/paid/
day/shade/away
❏ ring/boat/thing/float/in/shade/skin/suede/beach/blue/reach
/you/band/land
❏ least/conquest/then/man/that/spirit/powerful/pool/fornication/
insufflation/sun/carillion (or carillon)/home/wisdom

3. Write a sonnet suggested by another sonnet, an answer or an
extension of the argument.

4. Write a sonnet using assonance and/or consonance throughout instead of rhyme. No full rhymes – got it!

5. Many sonnets use an Alexandrine (six stresses) for the last
line. Edna St Vincent Millay used a seven-stress line there.
Write a sonnet (like Hopkins' 'The Windhover') **all** of whose
lines are not the traditional iambic pentameter but longer, as
with Hopkins, or shorter (tetrameter perhaps like Shakespeare's Sonnet 145), or alternating long and short.

6. Write a sonnet of seven couplets. The 17th century poet
Robert Herrick wrote one ('The Vision'), and Roy Fuller
does it more than once in his book-long sequence *Available
for Dreams*.

7. Write a sequence where each sonnet begins with the last line
of the previous one. The final line of the sequence is of course
a repeat of the opening one, thus giving the whole a pleasing
circular structure. A variation is not to repeat the lines until
the very end one, thus a sequence of three sonnets will not
have 42 lines, but only 40 (13 + 13 + 14) which is, far from
incidentally, the line limit for many competitions. Many
poetry competition judges, who are nearly always poets, are
professionally impressed by this kind of thing and I once
won £250 with such a sequence.

Haiku

Much loved by schoolteachers, because anyone can write a haiku who can recognise a syllable. Japanese haiku are a major art form and have all sorts of rules (I have a four-volume work on my shelves devoted to them), but the English kind have only one rule that matters; 17 syllables, usually divided into three lines in the proportion 5:7:5. 'Winter' is by Bill Devine:

> Fierce fast-freezing winds,
> Spidery etching on the panes,
> Season dark and harsh.

Some people call any little poem of three lines that neither rhymes nor scans a haiku, but I don't and neither should you. Titles are allowable, not mandatory.

> Five pints of Guinness,
> Seventeen bottles of Bass,
> Southern Comfort – aah!

This was a found poem, or at least an overheard poem. Japanese haiku are philosophical and elegiac but work well (perhaps better) as a light verse form – in English anyway. Then you could try a tanka (5:7:5:7:7):

> Five pints of Guinness,
> Seventeen bottles of Bass,
> Then Southern Comfort,
> Say half-a-dozen doubles,
> And (next day) Alka-Seltzer.

Clerihews

These were invented by Chesterton's boyhood friend, Edmund Clerihew Bentley. They are doggerel rhyming quatrains – the first line (sometimes the second) is made up of, or contains, the name of a famous person. Here are two:

> The poet Martial
> Was sexually impartial
> But everybody (and I mean *everybody*) swung both ways
> In the old Roman days.

> Jeremy Bentham
> When they played the Netional Entham
> Sat on
> With his hat on.

Long names that look difficult to rhyme give you a head start – John Betjeman, Count Dracula, Michelangelo Buonarotti.

Double dactyls

Were invented by the poets John Hollander and Anthony Hecht:

> Higgledy piggledy
> Alfred Lord Tennyson
> Liked to lie soaking for
> Hours in the tub,

> Hairy, horripilate,
> Hypochondriachal,
> Waiting for wifie to
> Give him a scrub.

It's true about the tub, untrue (I think) about the wife. The rules of a double dactyl are as follows

❑ The first three lines of each verse are double dactyls (/ . . / . .)
❑ The last line of each verse is a truncated double dactyl (/ . . /)
❑ Line 1 is a nonsense word (higgledy-piggledy, higamus-hogamus...)
❑ Line 2 is a proper name, usually a person
❑ Line 6 (occasionally line 5 or line 7) is a single word
❑ Line 4 rhymes with line 8.

Possible double-dactyl candidates would include Anna Karenina, Edward G Robinson, Marcus Aurelius, Franklin D (or Eleanor) Roosevelt, President Kennedy (or Eisenhower or Pompidou), General (or Colin) Montgomery…

Triolets

Triolets came in at the end of the 19th century, like a lot of other French forms. They have eight lines but only two rhymes. The first line is repeated twice and the second once: AbaAabAB, where the capital letters represent the repeated lines.

> We want ice cream,
> Stop at the shop.
> Stop or we'll scream
> Because WE WANT ICE CREAM!
> Summerlong dream
> With a cherry on top.
> We want ice cream,
> Stop at the shop.

Triolets are usually light and airy but don't have to be. Ruth Silcock wrote a series about a horrible children's home. Hardy wrote this:

The Puzzled Game-Birds

> They are not those who used to feed us
> When we were young – they cannot be –
> Those shapes that now bereave and bleed us?
> They are not those who used to feed us,
> For did we then cry, they would heed us
> – If hearts can house such treachery
> They are not those who used to feed us
> When we were young – they cannot be!

Changing the punctuation, and even some of the words, of the repeated lines is within the rules. Alan M Laing's poem in Chapter 3 is a triolet.

Villanelles

Wilde and Dowson wrote villanelles in the 1890s and, 50 years later, Dylan Thomas, William Empson and WH Auden wrote much better ones. There is a very fin-de-siècle example by Joyce in *The Portrait of the Artist as a Young Man*. They are generally six stanzas of iambic pentameter or tetrameter (Dowson has one in trimeter but it doesn't say much – it hasn't the space really) and rhyme A_1bA_2 abA_1abA_2 $abA_1abA_2abA_1A_2$, where A_1 and A_2 are repeated lines. They look impossibly difficult but they are not, not *impossibly*. Ann Drysdale's *Villanelle for Two Friends*:

> The nicest people seem to come in pairs
> And it's a double blessing when they do –
> A comely coupledom with no false airs.
>
> A private peace peculiarly theirs
> But which rubs off on other people too.
> The nicest people seem to come in pairs.
>
> A sort of self-sufficiency that shares
> Its comfort without even trying to.
> A comely coupledom, with no false airs;
>
> In ordinary day-to-day affairs
> Each bears in mind the other's point of view.
> The nicest people seem to come in pairs;
>
> An arithmetic paradox, which squares
> Their simple sum, creating something new –
> A comely coupledom with no false airs.
>
> Two people effortlessly holding shares
> In one another, like the two of you.
> The nicest people seem to come in pairs,
> A comely coupledom, with no false airs.

The best place to start is the repeated lines – which must be strong or the poem will fail. William Empson is particularly good at these.

Ballades

These were favourites of Chesterton and his friends, who wrote bucketloads. Good examples are Chesterton's 'Ballade of Suicide' and Belloc's 'Ballade of Genuine Concern'. Ballades are usually in iambic pentameter or tetrameter. Three eight-line stanzas all rhyming **ababbaba** (two rhymes) or **ababbcbc** (three rhymes), the last line of each is a refrain. A four-line envoi traditionally addresses a Prince but need not. The master is medieval French poet

Francois Villon: good translators of his Ballades are Swinburne, Norman Cameron and Robert Lowell. My favourite is Tom Scott's 'Ballat o the Leddies o Aulden Times', but I know how the English can be about Scots so I have chosen Swinburne, actually a variation with ten-line stanzas (**ababbccdcd**) and a five-line envoi:

The Epitaph in Form of a Ballad

Men, brother men, that after us yet live,
Let not your hearts too hard against us be;
For if some pity of us poor men ye give
The sooner God shall take of you pity,
Here are we five or six strung up you see,
And here the flesh that all too well we fed
Bit by bit eaten and rotten, rent and shred,
And we the bones grow dust and ash withal;
Let no man laugh at us discomforted,
But pray to God that he forgive us all.

If we call on you, brothers, to forgive,
Ye should not hold our prayer in scorn, though we
Were slain by law; ye know that all alive
Have not wit always to walk righteously;
Make therefore intercession heartily
With him that of a virgin's womb was bred,
That his grace be not as a dry well-head
For us, nor let Hell's thunder on us fall;
We are dead, let no man harry or vex us dead,
But pray to God that he forgive us all.

The rain has washed and laundered us all five,
And the sun dried and blackened, yea, perdie,
Ravens and pies with beaks that rend and rive
Have dug our eyes out, and plucked off for fee
Our beards and eyebrows; never are we free,
Not once, to rest; but here and there still sped,
Drive at its wild will by the wind's change led,
More pecked of birds than fruits on garden wall;
Men, for God's love, let no gibe here be said,
But pray to God that he forgive us all.

Prince Jesus, that of all art Lord and head,
Keep us that hell be not our bitter bed;
We have nought to do in such a master's Hall.
Be not ye therefore of our fellowhead,
But pray to God that he forgive us all.

It is interesting to compare this with a modern version, say that of the American, Robert Lowell. Lowell eschews archaism ('withal'), inversion ('Let not your hearts too hard against us be'), redundacy included for the metre ('men, brother men'), all probably gains. But Lowell makes things difficult for himself by shortening the line to a tetrameter (Villon's is pentameter), his metre is rougher (an effect Lowell liked), his translation looser and his rhymes sometimes forced (no-one is as acrobatic a rhymer as Swinburne). Both translations are good; neither is perfect, though Swinburne's refrain is, perhaps, very nearly so.

Sestinas

Fiendish – and French again. A successful sestina is a sort of advanced poetic test. Sestinas don't rhyme but use six end-words that repeat themselves in an arcane order. They have 39 lines (six stanzas of six lines each with a three-line envoi) and are thus suitable for all those poetry competitions with a 40-line limit. Let me work through *Red-Eye*:

> My red-eyed laughing barber cared but **little**
> What skulls he clipped, what chins & cheeks he **shaved.**
> My mother packed me off when I was **small,**
> Short back & sides she told him. He was **pale,**
> His slightly smaller left red-eye was **real,**
> He unscrewed the right right out when I was **older,**
>
> When the asymmetry made him look that much **older,**
> Then eased his pinkie, moistened with a **little**
> Vaseline over the unwinking glass, his **real**
> Left eye, red-eye, observing. I, half-**shaved,**
> My moony, mirrored face as pocky **pale**
> As a goat's cheese, I was watching too. Some **small**

If the repeated words in the first stanza are represented by **abcdef**, then the pattern in the second stanza is **faebdc** (last, first, second, last, second, third last, third). This order is not crucial, but having set it up in the second stanza the poet is supposed to stick to it through the next four.

> Probably venomous insect buzzed & I thought how **small,**
> How bright, how intricate as we grow **older,**

It shines, the old innocence beyond the **pale**.
We yearn back to the abandoned city, dinky **little**
Streets, warm intimate squares, well-**shaved**
Lawns & rank on rank of improbable flowers **real**

Life can never beat – what is as **real**
As your misremembered bliss at being **small**?
Why I used to watch my father while he **shaved**,
Asked could I strop the razor? When you're **older**.
But I won't want to do it then. You peel back **little**
Scans off your knees & the skin there, it's all **pale**,

It's shiny, not like proper skin, it's **pale**,
It's dead like paper, shiny & **unreal**.
Most nights I wake round four to **little**
Sighs & squeaks & settlings. Being **small**
Just stops being an option when you're **older**,
When the family needs you showered & shat & **shaved**,

It's a man thing see. My red-eyed barber **shaved**,
Talked, laughed and snipper-snippered. Moony, **pale**
Behind thick, drawn curtains something whispers: **older**,
Unwiser & twenty thousand times more **real**.
You've given away the job of being **small**
For ever friend, but you have to laugh a **little**.

The envoi brings back the words in their original order, two per half-line:

Red-eye, you laugh a **little** now you're **shaved**,
You carry your **small** guts round in a **pail**.
Nothing is **real**, you learn that when you're **older**.

The form is obsessional, slightly mad; the poems it generates tend to be that too. Spenser and Sidney wrote sestinas in the 16th century, Swinburne (who composed a double sestina and another one that actually *rhymes*) and Kipling ('Sestina of the Tramp-Royal' – one of his best poems) in the 19th, Pound and Auden (many times) in the 20th. A surprising number of modern poets, particularly Americans, have written sestinas – perhaps because they don't exactly *rhyme*, which many US poets seem to be against on principle. Or perhaps a lot of poets are mad obsessionals.

Pantoums

Malay, not French – though coming to us *through* French poets. Four-line stanzas rhyme **abab**; first and third lines are second and fourth lines of the preceding stanza. Like this:

> There's something horrid in the lake,
> Lulu knows and will not say.
> *Is Piccalilli still awake?*
> I hate it when she gets that way.
>
> Lulu knows, she will not say,
> She winds her hair and sucks her thumb,
> I hate it when she gets that way.
> I know the horrid thing will come.
>
> Lu winds her hair, she sucks her thumb,
> She says the moon is very bright.
> I know the horrid thing will come,
> I know that it will come tonight.
>
> I know the moon is very bright,
> I know the sky is very old,
> I know the thing will come tonight
> To wrap me in its scales of gold.
>
> The sky above is very old,
> The lake below is very deep.
> *O wrap me in your scales of gold*
> *And take me to your isles of sleep.*
>
> The lake down there is very deep,
> There's something horrid in the lake.
> *Please take me to your isles of sleep.*
> *Piccalilli's still awake.*

A pantoum can be of any length, but the last stanza winds it up by using as its second and fourth lines the first and third lines of the first stanza, thus making the poem perfectly circular. Traditionally the third and fourth lines of each stanza work out a separate theme from that of the first and second, but I have ignored that – as do Wendy Cope ('Roger Bear's Philosophical Pantoum') and Sophie Hannah ('Swimming Pool Pantoum') who says: 'I feel a set form, far from being restrictive, is very liberating and forces your imagination to explore possibilities it might not otherwise consider.' Quite.

Ghazal

Pronounced 'guzzle'. I discovered this Persian (and Arabic and Urdu) form in the poems of James Elroy Flecker. Ezra Pound asked rhetorically, 'Who reads Flecker now?' One answer is that I do, and more often than I read old Ezra:

Yasmin

How splendid in the morning glows the lily: with what grace he throws
His supplication to the rose: do roses nod the head, Yasmin?

But when the silver dove descends, I find the little flower of friends
Whose very name that sweetly ends I say when I have said, Yasmin.

The morning light is clear and cold: I dare not in that light behold
A whiter light, a deeper gold, a glory too far shed, Yasmin.

But when the deep red eye of day is level with the lone highway,
And some to Mecca turn to pray, and I toward thy bed, Yasmin;

Or when the wind beneath the moon is drifting like a soul aswoon,
And harping planets talk love's tune with milky wings outspread, Yasmin,

Shower down thy love, O burning bright! For one night or the other night
Will come the Gardener in white, and gathered flowers are dead, Yasmin.

A ghazal then, is a poem in couplets rhyming **ab cb db**, etc. Flecker's rather hypnotic triple internal rhymes are his own affair and you don't have to copy them – which is probably just as well. If you are following the Persian original, the first couplet should rhyme **aa**. Indeed it should do more than that; the rhymes throughout should be *rime riche*, (the same word repeated – as Flecker repeats the name Yasmin), and each couplet should be autonomous and disjunct (thematically different). No, I do not read Persian or Urdu or Arabic. I cribbed all that from John Hollander's *Rhyme's Reason* and Agha Shahid Ali in *The Practice of Poetry* edited by Robin Behn and Chase Twichell. But enough of this 'should'. We are writing English, not Persian, and we are magpies; we take what we like and leave what we like. In the US, according to Dana Gioia, poets are writing unrhymed ghazals (though I can't imagine what they would be like). Good ones have an intriguing, riddling quality, like Sophie Hannah's 'Ghazal' that begins:

> Imagine that a man who never writes
> Walks on the Planet Mars in cricket whites

Blues, calypsos and nashes

Stress is everything; syllables count for nothing. A blues:

> Woke up this morning, should have stayed in bed,
> Yes I woke up this morning, should have stayed in bed,
> Needed six fizzing alka-seltzer, just to ease my aching head.
>
> Devil's in the whisky, another devil's in the gin,
> Yes the devil's in the whisky and another devil's in the gin,
> There's ten thousand devils just laughing at the state I'm in.

And so on until you feel better, Both Auden and Ewart have tried their expert hands at calypsos but my favourite is still Lord Beginner's celebration of the West Indies' victory at Lord's in 1951. Two stresses to every line and as many syllables as you can fit in:

> **Calypso (Lord's 1950)**
>
> Cricket, lovely cricket
> At Lord's where I saw it,
> Cricket, lovely cricket
> At Lord's where I saw it,
> Yardley tried his best
> But Goddard won the Test.
> They gave the crowd plenty fun;
> Second Test and West Indies won.
> *With those two little pals of mine*
> *Ramadhin and Valentine.*

(Ogden) Nashes hark back to the first exercise in this boo, but a Nash is not true doggerel. The difference between Nash, the American and McGonagall, the Scot, is that Nash knew what he was doing.

> Perhaps when you tried that first exercise you were writing
>   McGonagallish trash
> But by now you are surely more of a Nash.

The lines of a Nash can be any length; they can (and perhaps they should) be very long indeed at times.

The only proviso is that you stick to your rhymes.

A Clerihew (qv) is, in essence, a Nash quatrain, though Nash himself didn't write any.

15. Getting it Writ then Getting it Right

Yeats, a great reworker and redrafter, insisted that the finished poem must, nevertheless seem the work of a moment. Byron pretended it *was* the work of a moment, but I don't believe him. You make poems the way Fred Astaire danced. Larkin wrote his in a notebook with a 2B pencil. I use a 2B pencil too; it is clear to see and easy to rub out. But mostly I use a PC. I like the way it shows me how the poem *looks* and lets me play around with the rhyme scheme, the line-endings, the order of the lines and the words inside the lines, the nuts-and-bolts of poem-assembly. It takes the idea of a poem as a little word machine about as far as it will go.

Doctor Johnson could compose up to 50 verses – what we call couplets – in his head. Gavin Ewart worked in much the same way; his drafts needed little revision once he got as far as writing them down in his neat, tiny script. But most of us like *written* drafts; we need something to look at.

You *should* be able to compose by the 2B pencil method. You have to sometimes, and it doesn't do to get fetishistic about a particular way of writing – often a convenient alibi for not writing at all. I find trains (I like trains) conducive to poetry, planes not (I am afraid of flying). A sonnet came to me in its entirety once on the tube journey from Richmond to Earls Court, which takes about half an hour. I wrote that down on the inside of a cigarette packet (one advantage of smoking I suppose) – nor am I the only person to have written verses on those tempting old white inserts.

Do you have a notebook? I have a hardcover A4 one with ruled lines and I do use it from time to time. I also use loose sheets of copier paper and any odd scraps, old till receipts, etc. There are always odd scraps. What there isn't always is a pencil, or at least a biro; that's something you must be sure always to have about you. I like a mechanical pencil that takes thick, soft leads and never needs sharpening. You get them in Art shops and I have two.

Why a notebook or at least a pencil and odd scraps? Because poems steal up on you and, if you don't nail them then, they may steal away again and be lost forever. Years ago when my daughter Ellie was a baby I spent many hours wheeling her up and down the streets where I live in the *very* early hours. If I stopped she would set up a wailing and wake the neighbours, so I didn't stop and composed poems about her by the Johnson method. I repeated short, rhyming stanzas over and over in my head, or even out loud (it was the middle of the night and a father with a baby has *carte blanche* to behave eccentrically). These poems form an entire section in a book and a reviewer said that their formal simplicity mirrored their content – quite so.

I don't do that now, though I still find the early morning is good. I am writing this at 5.05, a quiet time except for the cats sitting on or in front of the screen. (How do you stop them from doing that?)

Poets' drafts

It's fascinating and instructive to look at drafts of well-known poems, though some people – Charles Lamb was one – find it curiously unsettling that, say, Keats' opening to the 'Ode to a Nightingale':

> My heart aches and a drowsy numbness pains
> My sense

began as '… a painful numbness *falls*'. Or that the line in Blake's 'The Tyger':

> What dread hand? And what dread feet?

originally ran on into another stanza (heavily cancelled):

> What dread hand & what dread feet
>
> Could fetch it from the furnace deep
> And in thy horrid ribs dare steep
> In the well of sanguine woe
> In what clay & in what mould
> Were thy eyes of fury rolld
>
> What/where the hammer what/where the chain

A Shelley fragment begins unpromisingly:

> Ah time, oh night oh day
> ~~Ni na ni na, na ni~~
> ~~Ni na ni na, ni na~~
> Oh life O death, O time
>   Time a di
> ~~Never Time~~
> Ah time, a time O-time
>   ~~Time~~!

A later draft contains a long series of those na na na na syllables. He was working out metre and shape before he had words.

   Tennyson's 'Tithonus' begins in draft:

> Ay me! Ay me! The woods decay and fall,
> The vapours weep their substance to the ground,
> Man comes and tills the earth and lies beneath,
> And after many summers dies the rose.

The published version is much improved:

> The woods decay, the woods decay and fall,
> The vapours weep their burthen to the ground,
> Man comes and tills the field and lies beneath,
> And after many a summer dies the swan.

He has junked the over-plaintive opening, emended 'substance' with its intrusive sibilant s's to 'burthen'. The new word 'burthen' means three lisping 'th' sounds in one-and-a-half lines, so he alters the generalised 'earth' to the more particular 'fields'. 'Many-a-summer' achieves a momentary quickening of the line before the tolling hammer-blow of the transposed verb 'dies', and 'the rose' – straight out of poetic stock – has become, more unusually and therefore more memorably, 'the swan'. Better in at least three ways: swans are proverbially long-lived; they sing before they die, just as Tithonus is singing (though he is unable to die); and the chime of 'ground' and 'swan' makes the opening into the ghost, as it were, of a rhyming quatrain.

   A draft of Wilfred Owen's 'Anthem for Doomed Youth' contains not only his own revisions, but those of Siegfried Sassoon. Sassoon was older, already famous, and much admired by Owen; in spite of that, his amendments were usually rejected.

Sassoon, who did not care for the phrase 'holy music', suggested 'requiem' which Owen turned down, though it may have nudged him towards his final 'orisons' (which does have the advantage of rhyming with 'guns'). Owen's shells 'wail'; Sassoon wanted them to 'hiss' also. Presumably, since both men knew what they were talking about, shells both wailed and hissed. But shrill, demented wailing is all the noise they make in the final version, which I have printed on the right. You will also see that Owen's 'affinity with Keats' which Sassoon noted, extended to bad spelling:

Often, the difficult thing is to get the poem started at all. A manuscript of Edward Thomas' 'Adlestrop' shows he had a lot of difficulty with the first stanza; once that was right, the rest was easy. Here is that opening stanza (twice) with various corrections:

Anthem for Dead Youth	Anthem for Doomed Youth
passing	
What ~~minute~~ bells for those who die so fast?	What passing bells for those who die as cattle?
~~solemn~~ the	
Only the monstrous anger of ~~our~~ guns	Only the monstrous anger of the guns
blind insolence iron	
Let the ~~majestic insults~~ of ~~their iron~~ mouths	Only the stuttering rifles' rapid rattle
requiem	
Be as the ~~priest words~~ of their ~~burials~~	Can patter out their hasty orisons.
Learn organs for the old requiem	
	No mockeries no for them; no prayers nor bells
Of choristers and holy music, <u>none</u>;	Nor any voice of mourning save the choirs, –
And the hiss lonely	
~~The~~ long-~~drawn wail~~ of ~~high, far~~ sailing shells	The shrill, demented choirs of wailing shells;
t	
	And bugles calling for them from sad shires
to light	
What candles may we hold for these lost? ~~souls~~?	What candles may be held to speed them all?
Not in the hands of boys, but in their eyes	Not in the hands of boys, but in their eyes
shine the tapers the holy ~~tapers~~ candles	
Shall / many candles shine; ~~and love will light them~~	Shall shine the holy glimmers of good-byes
~~holy~~ flames: to	
And women's wide-spread~~ed~~ arms shall be their wreaths	The pallor of girls' brows shall be their pall
And pallor of girls' cheeks shall be their palls.	
~~mortal~~	
Their flowers the tenderness of ~~all men's~~ minds	Their flowers the tenderness of patient minds,
~~comrades~~	
rough men's	
each slow	
And every Dusk a drawing-down of blinds	And each slow dusk a drawing-down of blinds.
First ~~Draught~~ Draft	
(with Sassoon's amendments)	

Yes, I remember Adlestrop
At least the name, one afternoon
Of heat ~~the train slowed down~~ drew up there
~~There unexpectedly~~ Against its custom. It was ~~'twas~~ June.

Yes, I remember Adlestrop –
~~At least the name~~ The name, because One afternoon
Of heat, the express train drew up there
~~Against its custom~~ Unwontedly. It was late June.

And the published version:

Yes, I remember Adlestrop
The name – because one afternoon
Of heat the express train drew up there
Unwontedly. It was late June.

One problem with a PC is that, if you are not careful, you will lose your early drafts for ever and this is not a good idea. I am not talking about your ability to sell them to a university in Arizona for thousands of dollars when you are famous – though there is that – but you don't want to destroy *any* draft too soon. Second thoughts are not always best and besides, first thoughts *plus* second thoughts can often give you third or fourth thoughts. So save everything. Since there's room inside a PC for all the poetry Wordsworth ever wrote, in all the versions we have, there is *plenty* of room for alternative drafts of your sonnet. Larkin said he never threw anything out, and though there can be deep satisfaction in the occasional bonfire, I think he was probably right. One trouble with alternative versions is that you send the wrong one off, which, accepted, then becomes the right one – galling when you know it isn't.

Not just second thoughts . . .

The French poet, Paul Valery, said very truly that a poem is never finished, only abandoned. Nevertheless, you have to stop tinkering with it sometime and send it into the world to see if anybody else will love it, or at least to give it house-room. That is often hard to do, though it doesn't mean that you can't go back later for a little more tinkering if the result still doesn't satisfy.

Sometimes editorial rejection can actually help. I sent a sonnet to the late Alan Ross at *London Magazine*. He sent it back with a scribbled comment (he was good at scribbled comments) that the end wasn't quite right. I cursed inwardly but looked again. The poem described a school bully, whom I remembered particularly well (though he never gave me his individual attention) with a neat, clinching couplet suggesting that he had his problems too and to understand all is to forgive all. What was wrong with that?

Nothing at all, except that it wasn't true. I don't mean it wasn't true that he had his problems – doubtless he did. I met him later, a barman strangely diminished by life. I could 'forgive' him if I chose, but forgiveness was not what the poem was about. It was about cruelty and terror. Other school bullies were walking abroad; what right did I have to forgive them on behalf of their victims? Wasn't my forgiveness just a way of feeling good and safe? In short, the ending made the poem untrue *to itself*. As soon as I admitted this to myself I glimpsed another ending, the real one I had been too smug or cowardly to entertain. Perhaps I just did not want to contemplate my own abjectness at 12 years old. I wrote:

> And now? An ageing hardman, bald and fat?
> Dead in a ditch and damned? I'll drink to that.

I sent it off. Ross (bless him!) printed it. At other times I have resubmitted without the same happy result. Nevertheless, a writer should be open to criticism.

As TS Eliot was. He gave his manuscript of 'The Waste Land' to Ezra Pound who (among other things) wrote 'diffuse' more than once in the margins and Eliot cut his poem considerably, getting rid, in the process, of many traditional couplets and quatrains. What we have now is sharper, more Modernist, full of cinematic jump-cutting. Pound was an excellent editor for Eliot, better than for himself. Gavin Ewart makes the point succinctly: 'He took all the rubbish out of *The Waste Land*/And put it into *The Cantos*.' Good to have someone to take the rubbish out of one's own poems. For most of us that someone has to be our critical self. This is how you do it. Make the poem as good as you can, and leave it for a couple of weeks. Then you can see it with fresh eyes; if something is wrong, with luck, you will pick it up and be able to fix it.

Sometimes a poet fixes it after many months, even years. Wordsworth wrote his long autobiographical poem 'The Prelude' in 1805 and read it to Coleridge in the following year. But he didn't publish till 1850; by this time his opinions, literary and political, had shifted a long way and the two versions are very different. Sometimes a poet, Auden for example, rewrites after publication, which is hell for scholars. Which is the right poem? Are second thoughts always best? In Wordsworth's case often (though not always) they are not. But what about Yeats? We may think, and I do, that early lyrics published in the 1890s are considerably improved by revision and republication 40 years on.

Yeats, in a letter to Olivia Shakespeare, outlines a poem in terms so general it could be anything and sounds about as poetically promising as a shopping list. What he gets , after many, many drafts, is this:

> Speech after long silence; it is right –
> All other lovers being estranged & or dead,
> Unfriendly lamp-light his under its shade,
> The curtain drawn upon unfriendly night –
> That we descant & yet again descant
> Upon the supreme theme of art & song:
> Bodily decrepitude is wisdom; young
> We loved each other & were ignorant.

If ever there were a poet to whom poetry did not come naturally 'as leaves to a tree' in Keats' phrase, it was Yeats; his genius really was an infinite capacity for taking pains.

Exercise 25: Getting it right

Take a poem you never finished or have never been happy with. Try to look at it as if you have never seen it before. Don't think about *what you meant*; just look at *what you've got* – the words on the page. Is there anything promising or suggestive? What does it promise, what does it suggest? Perhaps it should go in a different direction. Perhaps it can be improved by cutting. One editor chopped the first stanza off one of my poems: nothing there that wasn't said better later, only I couldn't see it. You can get too close to your work; that is the point of putting it aside before the final draft.

Sometimes very little is worth saving. Robert Lowell looked over a poem submitted to him and said it really began with the last line. 'Just go on from there,' he suggested cheerfully. It would be good to know (wouldn't it?) which line that was. Look at your poem, decide which *is* the best line, then take a deep breath, abandon the rest and see where that line takes you.

The American poet Chase Twichell suggests you cut your poem up – yes, with scissors – and reassemble it in another way. Lynne McMahon suggests rewriting it in the negative. Try 'Shall I compare thee to a winter's night?'

Exercise 26: *From the sublime to the ridiculous*

There was a competition, I think in the *New Statesman*, to ruin a line of verse (to risible effect) by a single misprint – inspired, I think, by the line

Nothing is so beautiful as pring

(the ruined version of Hopkins' 'Nothing is so beautiful as spring'). Lines in Coleridge's 'The Ancient Mariner' are ruined to good effect:

Like a man who on a lonesome road
Doth walk in fear and dread
And having once turned round, walks on
And turns no more his head
Because he knows a frightful friend
Doth close behind him tread.

I hope you know that the original was 'fiend'.

Bare, ruined chairs where once the sweet birds sang

is from Shakespeare's Sonnet 73 (choirs).

For God's sake let us spit upon the ground

is from Richard II, or it was when the word was 'sit'. My favourite is what Claudius said to Hamlet before the fatal duel:

The King shall drink to Hamlet's better breath
And in the cup an onion shall he throw

Do you want to try? Isn't it sacrilege? Doesn't it dramatise for us that the most sublime poetry began with someone playing about with words?

Exercise 27: Alternative versions
Rewrite a poem in entirely different language. You could refashion an Elizabethan lyric in language suited to the 21st century, an exercise suggested by Sweeney and Hartley Williams. This is quite close to translation. If you are inclined to parody, you could employ some detestable jargon:

> The feasibility of drawing suggestive parallels between an equable and sympathetic disposition and mild meteorological conditions during a holiday period was considered but rejected on the following grounds: the uncertainty and brevity of such weather windows computes negatively with the lack of mood swings generally observable in a stable personality such as the one under discussion...

Or a song to a small guitar:

> You're like a day in summer,
>   My dear,
> But summer was a bummer,
>   This year...

16. Writing for Children

Children are overbearing, supercilious, passionate, envious, inquisitive, idle, fickle, timid, intemperate, liars and dissemblers; they laugh and weep easily, are excessive in their joys and sorrows, and that about the most trifling objects, they bear no pain but like to inflict it on others; already they are men.

Quoted by Stevie Smith in *Novel on Yellow Paper*

Or, as the poet, Jack Prelutsky, puts it – children are different from us, they have had fewer experiences and they are short. He goes on to say that children love to learn, and that is for the most part true. Certainly they are not defensive about what they know, like many adults; on the contrary, they are open to new ideas and new ways of seeing. They therefore should be, and are, splendid people to write for and I do like writing poems for children. I have had one book of them published and have enough material for another.

What *form*? Children's poetry books are not just the words on the page. Children's poetry publishers hope to make money, which adds a new dimension to the game. When I have a new book of adult poems I discuss it with Harry Chambers: we choose the poems, choose a cover and the book comes out to acclaim or derision or what the girl in the novel called 'complete ignoral'. The process is straightforward.

With a children's book things are different. It is better in this case – though very difficult – to find a big publisher because only they can do it with a low enough cover price. They do this by bringing out a number of titles simultaneously in the house format; this means a large print run and a low unit cost. They also use horrid, inferior paper. But at the time of writing, *The Complete Poetical Works of Phoebe Flood* retails at £3.50 and grown-up poetry books cost £7.99 or even £9.95, sums few children could persuade a parent to part with, not for a *poetry* book, dear me . . .

And the illustrator – a good illustrator can make a tremendous difference: Posy Simmons (Kit Wright), Quentin Blake (Roald Dahl, Michael Rosen). I possess and treasure Walter de la Mare's *Peacock Pie* illustrated by Heath Robinson, and Lauren Child who did my own book is terrific. Some poets illustrate their own books, but that is probably not a good idea unless your name is Mervyn Peake. Illustrators generally work for a fee rather than a royalty, which I think exploits them, but words in our culture always get preference over pictures and, since we are word people, I suppose that is to our advantage. At present big publishers have decided there is no money in single collections; anthologies are everything – they do tend to move in a phalanx one way or another, doubtless emailing one another through the long, dusty afternoons.

Selling children's poems is hard. Anthologists often send mail-outs to poets. How do you get on their lists? By publishing children's poems. How do you publish children's poems? By being on those lists.

What is a children's poem?

What about the poems you put *into* a children's book – how do you know they are children's poems? Absolutely the *wrong* way is to write *down* to your audience. A poem for a child is not a childish poem. There are poems that *cannot* be for children because they talk about things children do not know or use vocabulary they do not understand. But *all* children's poems should be capable of appealing to adults – who usually buy the book, after all – and they ought to appeal to you, the poet, in the first place. Don't leave your intelligence at the door when entering the house of childhood; the classic children's writers have an adult readership also. Harry Potter books come out in adult editions, identical except for the covers and a pound on the price.

The poet Matthew Sweeney deliberately mixes up the categories by sending off some children's poems to adult magazines. Sometimes I write a poem without being sure which category it fits until I have finished it and put it into the blue folder (grown-ups) or the red (children). Sometimes I switch folders. Some of the kiddiepo put out nowadays is low-pressure, hammering away at school, family, pets, ghosts, farting, rather relentlessly upbeat. I have written some myself and I'm not ashamed of it, but I do think the range could be extended a bit. The best poets do extend it.

What is a good children's poem? It must be interesting – interesting to real children that is, not to an adult idea of what a child is like or ought to be like. It should not preach; most of us can spot preaching when it is 100 years old, but there is plenty of preachy stuff around nowadays about racism, sexism, all kinds of isms. **Don't try to improve children.** Who are you that you should improve them? Interest them.

How can you do this? You *can* say bum a lot. That is the trap you fall into trying to avoid writing goody-goody poems for weedy Walter (Walter is a character in Dennis the Menace, and if you do not know him then probably you should steer clear of this chapter and this whole subject altogether). Don't aim at Walter, but don't aim exclusively at Dennis either. Sucking up to the kids at the back is probably a self-defeating tactic; you are not one of them, or you are not *just* one of them. Children consistently say in surveys that they like X and Y, and of course they do. But children will also say what those powerful in their world want them to say, and the powerful include real-life Dennis the Menaces and Minnie the Minxes, opinion-formers amongst their peers. In other words, they say they like what they feel they *ought* to like and in this way they are no different from the rest of us.

So give children your best. Frankly, when I started I did not invariably do this. I drove off some poems into the children's corral because they had not quite made it; they had imperfections that I could see but that kiddywinks would not. Or so I thought.

Wrong of course. If you read your poems aloud you will soon find which are the good ones. Children won't throw things or catcall, not in school with the teacher's eye on them, but they will withdraw their attention. Why not? Someone who goes to a poetry reading has at least connived at being bored. But children have to go to school, and if poets ambush them there they have no escape. I remember my own daughter (a nifty rhymer) home from school and telling me: 'We had a poet today.' I asked, 'How was he?' She rolled her eyes. 'Showing off. I think he'd forgotten what it was like to be a child.'

If you have forgotten what it was like to be a child then certainly you should not be a children's poet, perhaps not a poet at all – we ought surely to be remembering all sorts of people. On the other hand, this is what the children's writer Maurice Sendak has to say about his memories of childhood.

150

> People think I have some magic link to my childhood. If there is
> such a link, it's a process that by-passes my conscious mind,
> because I have very little real recollection. I couldn't stop and tell
> you why I'm writing and drawing certain episodes; they're coming
> from some inner source that does recollect.

But in another part of the same essay he says that he realised, as
he was drawing them, that the fierce creatures in his picture book
Where the Wild Things Are were his Jewish relatives.

Do you have to *like* children? I suppose if you can't stand them,
if the very sight of them drives you up the wall, then you would
be unwise to try and write for them. But a famous child-hater,
Philip Larkin – the man who suggested a Herod's Eve to follow
Halloween, during which bands of adults would roam the streets
and beat the daylights out of any child they came across – has
written poems which consistently, and rightly, find themselves in
children's anthologies. Lewis Carroll hated 50% of children – all
the boys. And I don't like children – not all of them. Some are
charming, most are alright, some ought to have been strangled at
birth. The person who says 'you should always believe a child',
and the other person who says 'little liars, all of them!' are both
indulging in child-ism; that is they are lumping all children
together in an agglomerate.

Don't write for *children*. Write for a child, the child you once
were, because that is the only child you really know. Of course the
children who are to hand (as your buried self is not) are a good
source for checking, and you have to mind your language. By that
I mean you have to talk to them in the language they use. But not
too insistently and not *all* the time. Right at the beginning of *The
Tale of Peter Rabbit*, Beatrix Potter uses the word 'soporific'
which most children, and some adults, will not know. A poem of
mine contains the words 'nard', 'Scheherezade' and 'cryptic'. I
used to avoid reading it for that reason, but I have recently tried
it out without any explanation and the hard words don't seem to
bother anybody. Children are always coming across words they
do not know (how else do they increase their vocabularies?) and
do not have to fully understand everything they read. It may be
exciting not to fully understand.

A children's writer once said to me: 'Forget about trying to write
for *all* children. Half of them don't read books so you're not going
to get to them.' That struck me as slightly shocking, but I think she

was right. Don't aim too low in an effort to mop up everybody. If you do then you will just be what my daughter called *silly*.

Who are the good children's poets? Alan Ahlberg and Michael Rosen are out in front in every kind of survey. So are Matthew Sweeney, Jackie Kay, Roger McGough, Charles Causley, John Mole and Wendy Cope. My favourite children's *poet* is Kit Wright (children like him too). My favourite children's *poem*s are Walter de la Mare's 'The Song of the Mad Prince' and quite a lot of Lewis Carroll - say this:

> 'The time has come', the Walrus said,
>   'To talk of many things:
> Of shoes - and ships - and sealing wax
>   Of cabbages - and kings -
> And why the sea is boiling hot -
>   And whether pigs have wings.'

Do children like that? Yes they do. They also like (and not necessarily just the thoughtful ones) 'The Highwayman' by Alfred Noyes, 'A Smuggler's Song' by Rudyard Kipling ('Watch the wall, my darling, while the Gentlemen go by'), 'Stopping by Woods on a Snowy Evening' by Robert Frost and 'The Trees' by Philip Larkin. And they like pretty well anything for children by Hilaire Belloc or Roald Dahl. Verbal violence allied with neat rhyming always goes down well. I loved the *Ruthless Rhymes* of Harry Graham and a verse my granny would recite:

> Mama, Mama, oh what is this
> That looks like strawberry jam?
> Hush, hush, my dear, 'tis poor Papa
> Run over by a tram.

Rhyming

Some people nowadays, as I think I said before, are snooty about rhymes. Not children though. Wendy Cope did a book of finger-rhymes for small children (she was a teacher of primary school children for years). And those great repositories of oral poetry, playground rhymes, go on for ever.

> Cowardy, cowardy custard
> Your face is made of mustard

Happy Birthday to you
Squashed tomatoes and stew

Oh my finger, oh my thumb,
Oh my belly, oh my bum

All to be heard in today's playgrounds and the children think they were made yesterday.

Exercise 28: Short, easy words

Write a short poem (say ten lines) using words that a child (say eight) would know. Do not tailor your poem to your idea of a child's experience.

Now introduce *one* difficult word like Beatrix Potter's 'soporific' or my 'nard'. Nard is an exotic oriental perfume if you didn't know, and I have no idea what it smells like. If your word was 'symmetry' then you might have this:

Tyger! Tyger! burning bright
In the forests of the night,
What immortal hand or eye
Could frame thy fearful symmetry?

You don't think eight-year-olds would know 'immortal'? Of course they would. Fantasy comics are full of it. A poem employing a simple vocabulary is not necessarily a simple poem. This is by Emily Dickinson:

I'm Nobody! Who are you?
Are you – Nobody – Too?
Then there's a pair of us?
Don't tell? they'd advertise – you know!

How dreary – to be – Somebody!
How public – like a Frog –
To tell one's name – the livelong June –
To an admiring Bog!

17. Other Ways of Speaking: Dialect and Nonsense

Feed Ma Lamz

Amyir gaffirz Gaffir. Hark.

> nay fornirz ur communists
> nay langwij
> nay lip
> nay laffn ina Sunday
> nay g.b.h. (septina wawr)
> nay nooky huntn
> nay tea-leaven
> nay chanty rasslin
> nay nooky huntn nix doar
> nur kuvitn their ox

Oaky doaky. Stick way it
– rahl burn thi lohta yiz.

Alas, to some this is nonsense. We Southern English do tend to assume dialect is silly, and people should just snap out of it. Of course what we speak can't be dialect – it's normal. This attitude surfaces when a Scot gets to read the news.

Of course, Scots wouldn't call what they speak a dialect – it's a *language*, with a dictionary from the Aberdeen University Press. It may be – that depends on how you define a language – but it isn't different from English in the way that French is. And French isn't different from English in the way that Chinese is. I think both the Scots and the English like to exaggerate linguistic differences; I also think that is a pity. We don't appreciate Burns (almost as good as the Scots make out); we don't know Dunbar, whose 'Lament for the Makars' is one of the 20 great poems in the language (which language, I won't say); we don't know Henryson's 'Testament of Cresseid' or the Border Ballads, or Fergusson or Garioch or Soutar, or MacDiarmid. Tom Leonard, the national treasure who wrote the Decalogue above, is a closed book. OK, I didn't get 'chanty rasslin' either (though a 'chanty' is a chamber pot).

At least the Scots are not supposed to be stupid, unlike, say, Dorset hayseeds. In the National Portrait Gallery is a portrait of 'William Barnes (1801–1886), Scholar and Artist. Famous for his poetry in the Dorset dialect. Rector of Winterbourne Came, 1862'. Barnes in a long white beard, a soft hat and a smock, looks no odder to us than Tennyson, but you may not know his poetry.

Childhood

Aye, at that time our days wer but vew,
An our lim's wer but small, an a-growen;
An then the feair worold wer new,
An' life wer all hopevul an' gay;
An' the times o' the sprouten o' leaves,
An the cheak-burnen seasons o' mowen,
An' binden o' red-headed sheaves,
Wer all welcome seasons o' jay.

Then the housen seem'd high that be low,
An' the brook did seem wide that is narrow,
An' time, that do vlee, did goo slow,
An' veelens now feeble wer strong,
An' our worold did end wi' the neames
O' the Sha'sbury Hill or Bulbarrow;
An' life did seem only the geames
That we played as the days rolled along!

Unlike Dorset, Caribbean dialects have made it poetically. Roger Garfitt in _Poetry Review_ claimed for them a status above Scots, which he seemed to think just a matter of funny spelling. Humph! Nevertheless, Grace Nicholls, John Agard and others write well. This is from 'The Limbo Walkers' by Maggie Harris:

ah siddung wit mih fadda by the rivuh
he dead dead   we know dat
the berbice watas wetting he feet not mine

ah point mih finguh cross the oddah side
traveller dem lining up and waiting
the wata she licking dem toe slow slow.

In case you should be fazed by this, she includes a translation – in fact she begins with 'correct' English:

> I sit with my father by the river
> He is dead. We both know that
> The Berbice river wets his feet, not mine.

which has less vivacity, don't you think?

Kingsley Amis translated Rimbaud into cockney. Our incredulity (can the man be serious?) neatly makes his point that some dialects are low status – cockney belongs to taxi-drivers and is therefore unsuitable for 'serious' poetry. Again humph! Is 'Villon's Straight Tip' – WE Henley's turn of the century version of Villon's 'Tout aux tavernes et aux filles' – a 'serious' poem?:

Suppose you screeve? or go cheap-jack?	write begging-letters	be a pedlar
Or fake the broads? or fig a nag?	work the 3-card trick	dope a horse
Or thimble-rig? or nap a yack?	play 'find the lady'	steal a watch
Or pitch a snide? or smash a rag?	pass counterfeit coin	ditto banknotes
Suppose you duff? or nose and lag?	sell smuggled goods	be an informer
Or get the straight, and land your pot?	get a good tip and have a big win	
How do you melt the multy swag?	spend the big money	
Booze and the blowens cop the lot.	drink and tarts	

Fiddle, or fence, or mace, or mack;	swindle	pimp
Or moskeneer, or flash the drag;	pawn fraudulently	rob from vehicles
Dead-lurk a crib, or do a crack;	steal by deception	steal by force
Pad with a slang, or chuck a fag;	commit highway robbery	give up honest work
Bonnet, or tout, or mump and gag;	cheat	beg
Rattle the tats, or mark the spot;	use loaded dice	marked cards
You cannot bank a single stag;	shilling	
Booze and the blowens cop the lot.		

Suppose you try a different tack,		
And on the square you flash your flag?		
At penny-a-lining make your whack,	journalism	
Or with the mummers mug and gag?	acting	
For nix, for nix the dibs you bag!	money	
At any graft, no matter what,		
Your merry goblins soon stravag:	cash	wander
Booze and the blowens cop the lot.		

It's up the spout and Charley Wag	playing truant	
With wipes and tickers and what not	handkerchiefs	watches
Until the squeezer nips your scrag,	noose	neck
Booze and the blowens cop the lot.		

Burns often felt defensive about Scots. In 'To a Mouse' ('Tae a Moose'?) he alternates stanzas in Scots and English, keeping his English for the more philosophical (and boring) bits. MacDiarmid saw this as selling out. Maybe, but many Scots are double-tongued, talking English in the lecture room and Scots in the bar.

That surely goes for West Indians and others as well. It's true that written-down dialect can smell of the lamp. MacDiarmid's Lallans is a synthetic language: nobody, as he admits himself, ever spoke like that; and even Scots need a glossary. But all poetry is synthetic, isn't it? 'My heart aches, and a drowsy numbness pains my sense' – whoever spoke like that?

American? Australian? South African?

Is American a dialect of English? Or is English a dialect of American? Because of Hollywood and American pop, most of us have a goodish working knowledge of American, but the converse seems not to be true (perhaps connected with the observable fact that most American actors can't do accents) and many a British film needs subtitles before it can be understood over there. We all know about problems with phrases like 'I could do with a fag', and 'Would you mind knocking me up in the morning?'

Perhaps the word dialect brings with it un-useful ideas about correctness and deviation from a norm. There is no norm. RP (Received Pronunciation, meaning Upper Middle Class Southern English) is dead – or dead as a norm. It is alive as a dialect.

Vertical dialects

As I hinted in my remarks about Cockney, dialects are not only geographical (horizontal) they also move up and down the social scale (they are vertical). Betjeman's famous 'How To Get On In Society' works because of the differences between 'U' (upper-class) and 'non-U' speech and behaviour in England in the 1950s. 'Are the requisites all in the toilet?' asks the non-U speaker – non-U *words* are 'requisites' and 'toilet'. Betjeman gets in about 20 others – serviette, lounge, comfy, couch (couch!), sweet, etc. These should be (I think) lavatory, napkin, sitting room, sofa (settee is non-U, too) and pudding. There are also lots of non-U *things* – electric logs, cruets, doileys ... Do *you* say 'toilet'? I don't (it was drummed into me not to), but my children do, so perhaps we English are growing out of it at last.

Exercise 29: Speaking my language

Perhaps another version of Exercise 27. Take a poem or part of a poem that you like and translate it into the dialect of your choice. You may have to make changes that are other than purely verbal. For example, a cockney version of Gray's 'Elegy' would have to be in a town churchyard: curfew, herd and ploughman would have to be urbanised. Kit Wright has written 'A Clubman's Ozymandias' (So this chap tells this other chap/ Some damned claptrap/About how somewhere on the old map/He's seen these de-bagged legs . . .); Roger Crawford does Liverpool ('busies' are taxi-drivers):

> An there will be time
> Fer me to go meet me peergroup in the dump;
> Ter roll a drunk or give some cow a hump
> An time ter wire another horseless carriage
> Or have a gangshag in a broke-in garage
> Time ter do what we goan ter do
> Before we sit round sniffing bags of glue
>
> In twos an twos the busies comes an goes
> Chattin back ter their radios

Dialect may look like nonsense to some. But true nonsense is a dialect of its own.

'Elephants are contagious': nonsense and surrealism

> Bumble, bumble, bumbledom,
> Buzz, buzz, buzz.
> Stumble bumble, tumble bumble,
> Buzz buzz buzz.
> Rumble bumble, grumble bumble,
> Buzz buzz buzz,
> Fumble bumble, mumble bumble,
> Buzz buzz buzz.

That is about bees I think; it is certainly about something. Nonsense that is simply non-sense will not do; it must seem (or at least look like) sense and the patterning of poetry is one way to make it so.

Ring-a-ring-a-roses
A pocket full of posies
Atishoo atishoo
We all fall down

Robert Graves says that's about the Great Plague, but children
don't know that, and assigning a 'meaning' does not make it better
poetry. Dylan Thomas:

The first poems I knew were nursery rhymes, and before I could
read them for myself I had come to love just the words of them, the
words alone. What the words stood for, symbolised, or meant, was
of very little importance; what mattered was the sound ...

Yet Graves is right; few Nursery Rhymes began as nonsense.
'Sometimes the nonsense element has been added later, either
because the original words were garbled or forgotten, or because
they had to be suppressed for political or moral reasons.' Who
were the Grand Old Duke of York, Little Jack Horner, the Lion
and the Unicorn? Read 'Mother Goose's Lost Goslings' in *The
Crowning Privilege* and you will know.

Deliberately nonsensical rhymes for children first appeared in the
eighteenth century, as a reaction against the over-decorous verse of
the over-sane Augustan Age, and even these were a fairly restrained
sort of nonsense, based on puns and manifest self contradiction. It
was not until the time of Edward Lear and Lewis Carroll that
nonsense of brilliant inconsequence studded with newly invented
words came to be composed.

Nonsense (rather than simply non-sense) is contemporary with the
Romantic invention of Childhood (not, of course, with the
invention of children). Small children love nonsense but they lose
their taste for it as they grow into bigger children and begin to
make sense of the world. Then they prefer puzzles. I first read this
when I was about 11 and could make nothing of it.

I saw a peacock with a fiery tail
I saw a blazing comet drop down hail
I saw a cloud wrapped with ivory wand
I saw an oak creeping upon the ground
I saw a pismire swallow up a whale
I saw the sea brimful of ale

I saw a Venice glass full fifteen feet deep
I saw a well full of men's tears that weep
I saw red eyes all of a flaming fire
I saw a house bigger than the moon and higher
I saw the sun at twelve o'clock at night
I saw the man that saw this wondrous sight

When I was shown the solution – that you stop, or start, in the middle of each line – I was satisfied and liked the poem. Now that I am older, the key matters less to me than the romantic images – a well of tears, a house bigger than the moon; the surreal images – 15-foot glass, a sea of ale; and the horrific images – a creeping oak, eyes of fire. Incidentally, the date of this is given as 1671, which mean that it fits Graves' thesis in only *looking like* nonsense.

Poets need a strain of nonsense in their compositions, otherwise their poems will plod. You have to be a 'foot-off-the-ground person', as Stevie Smith puts it, or at least encourage the foot-off-the-ground part of yourself. When does nonsense become surreal? Possibly when we are looking for an adult audience and need a long French word to make our nonsense respectable. *Sur* is Latin *super* (above, beyond); so *Sur*realism is something beyond, or better than, realism.

Exercise 30: A surreal five minutes

The first literary Surrealists (they flourished in the 1920s) were fond of automatic writing, something you can try too. You sit with a pencil and paper, or in front of a computer screen, and write down whatever comes into your mind as quickly as you can and for a fixed, short period of time – say five minutes. It is quite a good idea to pick a subject. This can, and perhaps should, be done at random by opening a dictionary and looking at, say, the tenth word down – which will undoubtedly turn out to be something like Teguexin (a mexican lizard) and probably quite unsuitable. However, lizard would do – so get on with it.

Those early Surrealists assumed that what you got was an upwelling of the unconscious mind and therefore a *pure act of creation*, holy and not to be tampered with. 'Elephants are contagious' is a proverb created in this way by the French poet Paul Eluard, but, truthfully, not much pure automatic writing is as felicitous as this. Later Surrealists took to doctoring the

---

original evidence with their conscious minds and I think they were right. Never drive a theory further than it will go.

You could spend your five minutes writing down whatever new, nonsensical proverbs come into your head. If elephants are contagious, then perhaps antelopes are parsimonious, lizards are impossible and lobsters are sinful. Some of this might lead to poetry created with the conscious mind, like this double dactyl:

> Lobsters are sinful,
> They swallow a skinful
> Then stagger home sideways
> And beat up their kids.
>
> 'Learn to behave!' they cry
> Incomprehensibly.
> That is why lobsters are
> All on the skids.

There is a surreal exercise I learned from Wendy Cope, a version of which can be found in *Writing Poetry and Getting It Published* by Matthew Sweeney and John Hartley Williams. This is how I do it. You need quite a lot of people, at least eight, for it to work with total success.

Exercise 31: The elated taxi
Distribute sheets of unlined A4 paper – copy paper is good. Fold your paper three times each both ways so that when you open it out again you get 64 rectangles like this:

1. Fill in all eight rectangles in the first column with the word 'the'. Fold it over so that what you have written is invisible. I know that sounds silly because everyone has written the

same thing, but you are getting into a rhythm. Pass your paper to your left-hand neighbour.

2. You have received a paper from your right-hand neighbour. Fill in the second column with eight adjectives of your choice. Fold and pass left.

3. Take the new paper from your right and fill in the third column with eight nouns – abstract, concrete, whatever you like. Fold and pass left.

4. Continue with eight transitive verbs (verbs that take a direct object), fold and pass left. Then eight 'the's (fold and pass left), eight more adjectives and eight more nouns. Always fold and pass left. You will receive at last (from your right) a paper with seven columns filled in. Ignore the eighth.

If any verb is *not* transitive, now is the time to put that right with a well-chosen preposition. With any luck, you will have eight surreal sentences of this kind:

The	Elated	Taxi	Toasted	the	Napoleonic	Mouse	
The	Sexy	Investment	Sank	The	Cardboard	President	

This works well with children, provided that they are at least ten years old (otherwise they will have trouble with nouns/adjectives/transitive verbs). Adults tend to fail the paper-folding bit.

Dylan Thomas' habit of dealing out adjectives for his poems from a notebook, listing them according to their sound values and syllabic count rather than their meanings, obviously has some resemblance to this game. So does one of the great 20th century poems – Wallace Stevens' 'Sea Surface Full of Clouds'.

Exercise 32: The time, the place, the thing

Here is a variation tried with a class of ten-year-olds:

TIME OF DAY	PLACE	AND THE THING	IS DOING SOMETHING
Seven o'clock	in the palace	and the octopus	is on fire
Teatime	in the submarine	and the gerbils	are all reading The Beano
?	?	?	?

Judicious doctoring produced:

Morning in the jungle
& the ham-sandwiches
are lying in wait,

Twilight in Hell
& the devils
have just come in from cricket practice,

Night-time in the wardrobe
& my shirts
are holding a séance.

Most of the children did not know the word 'séance', but one did, the one who wrote the line.

18. The Art of Coarse Poetry Reading

I was recently at the Purcell Room on London's South Bank for a poetry reading. £7.00 bought me three poets, each one reading for around 40 minutes. The splendid Ursula Fanthorpe did her Hinge and Bracket act with Dr Rosie Bailey, and Michael Donaghy, all of whose poems were new to me, was crisp, witty and *without a book*. Enter Les Murray wearing a baseball cap and an enormous technicolour pullover (with other things like trousers of course), his book and his glasses in a carrier bag. He took off the cap, mislaid the glasses and, after the briefest of opening remarks, read with just the occasional aside. There was nothing remotely actorly about it – he even lost his place once – and he held the audience (fans admittedly) in the palm of his hand through the power of his words and the power of his personality.

I have been to other readings – readings where a poet muttered into a sleeve or ranted to the rafters, readings where a poet couldn't wait to scuttle back down whatever hole he or she came out of, where a poet *continually* lost the place, couldn't decide which poem to read next, had obviously spent the previous couple of hours in a pub. I have been to the worst kind of reading of all, where you can't get the poet off the stage again.

I have also given readings, on my own or with others. I have read at a Garden Festival where the organisers decided that Sylvia Kantaris and I could declaim in the open like Bible-bashers. Not possessing the Ancient Mariner's glittering eye, we adjourned fairly smartly to the tea tent. The fee was hard to get, too. I have actually refused to read because, though there were many performers, there was no audience; the organiser forgot to put up posters. I have read in a beautiful 18th century Edinburgh room to two men, no three men and a dog – the third man was the friend who brought me. I have read where the microphone boomed. I have read where the microphone sparked, I have read where the microphone failed to do anything at all. I have sermonised from the pulpit in a church with an echo like Fingal's Cave to a scattered dozen, the nearest a good 50 yards distant. I have read to 300 children in a school gymnasium without benefit of any public address system at all. I have read in a Donegal pub where the audience began turning up in ones and twos an hour after the advertised time (real coarse poetry reading, I suppose). That one went with a swing, courtesy of Messrs Guinness, Beamish, Jamieson and Bushmills until the poetry-lovers staggered out into the starlit night to wreak automotive havoc on the local sheep population. No, I lie: quick on their feet, are Irish sheep.

And I have read to appreciative audiences in sympathetic surroundings, answered questions, sold and signed books afterwards, talked in an agreeable bar and gone home full of good food and good wine, with my pockets jingling with money.

Reading your poetry: what to do

- ❏ *Know how long* you are going to read for. Ask the organiser and stick to what you are told. All venues ought to be supplied with a Music Hall hook with which to jerk off the stage poetasters who overstay their welcome.
- ❏ Know *how much* you are going to read. Remember that your audience would like to know about you and about your poems. And they can't read any one of your poems; they hear it and they hear it only once. So they need help. Six or seven poems well read, each with its own preamble, will be better received than a dozen galloped through. Poetry is like marmite – good spread thin.
- ❏ Know *which* poems you are going to read and *where* they are. Riffling through a book for a poem and then not finding it is a sure way of losing an audience.
- ❏ Mix it up. Flank a long poem with two short ones, a difficult poem with two easy ones. Do not be relentlessly serious. Do not be relentlessly jokey either.
- ❏ Speak *loudly* and *slowly*. I don't mean you should bawl at a funereal pace but don't forget Walter Pater asking assembled students whether they had heard him. 'We overheard you,' Oscar Wilde shouted back. Don't be overheard.

- ❏ Do not read cold. Practise beforehand. Michael Donaghy has memorised all his poems. It is not necessary to go so far but move in that direction.
- ❏ Do not be drunk.

Undoubtedly there are some poems (and indeed some poets) that go over well at readings, and these are not necessarily the best ones. Tennyson's 'Charge of the Light Brigade' would read splendidly, much better than 'Locksley Hall' (too long). Actors will tell you that *Richard III* is much easier to perform than *Macbeth*. You need some rousing poems that say obvious things obviously. If you haven't written any, then perhaps you should have. But any poem will communicate some of its magic if the reader will just let it. You must have confidence in your own lines; if you truly think they need dressing up, then you do not think enough of them. Beware of 'acting', by which I mean overacting.

Where is it written that you *must* do poetry readings? Larkin didn't, or he didn't very often, though he was a good reader. Dylan Thomas, a real rabble-rouser, was dismissive about his performances, 'reading out in my plummy voice poems that could be better understood in a book'. Kingsley Amis came to the launch party of *Making Cocoa for Kingsley Amis*, but left before the reading, 'so as not to break the habit of a lifetime'.

Actors are often appalling readers, as any poet will know who has heard one of his or her babies strangled in its cradle by some relentless thespian. On the other hand, if you have never heard Richard Burton read Gerard Manley Hopkins, you have missed something truly life-enhancing. Come to that, if you have never heard Burton read any verse at all, then you should. Another marvellous reader was Ted Hughes, both of his own work and of other poets, particularly TS Eliot. Seamus Heaney is a good reader, and Robert Graves was. The American poet and mortician Thomas Lynch knows how to deliver a line. On the other hand, to my ear, Yeats and Tennyson murdered their muse with a high bardic keening – though there is a certain amount of fashion in such things.

> Fame is the spur that the clear spirit doth raise
> (The last infirmity of noble mind)
> To scorn delights and live laborious days ...

John Milton: 'Lycidas'

Exercise 33: Read it aloud

When you have written a poem then *read it aloud*. To whom? To yourself. To a recording machine. To Emily Dickinson's admiring bog? Roald Dahl's grandchildren recounted how he used to read what he had written to them, hot off the press, as it were. He did not want their opinion, and they were much too much in awe to give it, but he wanted to know how his work sounded. Try reading a poem in different ways – aggressively, confidingly, sneeringly, sweetly like your old granny. Ham it up. This is to stop you hamming it up in public. Where? The bath is a good place – there's something about the acoustic. You want to know how it sounds.

19. Rich and Famous

'Now you are a romantic,' said Father Brown. 'For instance, you see someone looking poetical and you assume he is a poet. Do you know what the majority of poets look like? What a wild confusion was created by that coincidence of three good-looking aristocrats at the beginning of the nineteenth century; Byron and Goethe and Shelley! Believe me, in the common way, a man may write: "Beauty has laid her flaming lips on mine", or whatever that chap wrote, without being particularly beautiful. Besides, do you realise how old a man generally is, before his fame has filled the world?'

GK Chesterton: 'The Scandal of Father Brown'

Anyone can be rich; win the lottery jackpot. Anyone can be famous; get abducted by aliens. Or you could try writing poetry.

Shakespeare got quite rich and very famous indeed by writing poetry. The riches he actually enjoyed during his lifetime, quite a lot of the fame too, for many celebrated poets threw poems into his grave and they wouldn't have done that for a nobody. It is also worth repeating that Shakespeare was not a graduate, indeed we have no *record* that he even went to school. Other famous poets without a university education include the learned Ben Jonson, (Doctor Samuel Johnson went to Oxford, though he never graduated), Pope, Keats, Burns, Blake, Browning, Yeats, Dylan Thomas and practically any woman you care to name before our present age. But poets are bookish people and the list of Oxbridge graduates is long: Marlowe, Donne, Milton, Marvell, Dryden, Wordsworth, Coleridge, Byron, Tennyson, Sylvia Plath and Ted Hughes from Cambridge. Eliot, Auden, MacNeice, Graves, Larkin, Betjeman ('failed in Divinity'), Alan Brownjohn, James Fenton, Wendy Cope from Oxford. And plenty I have forgotten.

Often learned but rarely rich. I heard on Desert Island Discs (so it must be true) that the Oxford Professor of Poetry, James Fenton, made a million by writing poems – lyrics for Cameron Mackintosh's smash hit-musical *Les Miserables*, though I don't think they were ever used. But most poets are poorer than the average doctor or the average solicitor – which is as it should be, don't you think?

So rich and famous is likely to translate into just rubbing along and known to some people, with a few published books, fewer of them actually in print. Are you happy with that? How do you get to do it?

Start young

'I lisped in numbers, for the numbers came', wrote Alexander Pope, and by numbers he meant verses, poetry. Writing poems as a child is certainly a good start, though the poems *don't have to be any good*. Poets are rarely prodigies; the only ones I can think of are Dylan Thomas (the Rimbaud of Cwmdonkin Drive) and the great Arthur himself. Rimbaud published his first book at 16, ran away to Paris, had a hectic affair with another, older poet, Verlaine, got shot by him (he had it coming, believe me) and repudiated poetry for ever at 19. The rest of his life he travelled the world as a mercenary, an explorer, a trader in slaves and guns. He lost a leg to a crocodile and died, probably as a result, at the age of 37. Thomas' career, though less spectacular (and what wouldn't be?), has certain points in common. He lived a rackety life, died before he was 40 and most of his poetry seems to have been written before he was out of his teens.

The best young poet of the last 20 years is Sophie Hannah. I met her when she was just 22 on a writing course where she wrote a publishable (and later published) poem in an hour and a half! Three books of poems already and she still isn't 30 (novels too!). I asked her how many poems she had out 'doing the rounds' of magazines and competitions. She thought. 'Seventy,' she said. Good Lord!

Start old

But, in spite of the popular picture of the poet as an eternal teenager, these early birds are really exceptions; late-starters outnumber them. Kirkpatrick Dobie's first book came out when that poet was well over 80. I think that is the record until someone tells me different.

The most famous Victorian poem (if you forget about 'The

Charge of the Light Brigade') is probably 'The Rubaiyat of Omar Khayyam', a free translation – or an 'imitation' as the modern poets say – of the medieval Persian by Edward Fitzgerald. Fitzgerald did not complete his first version (he was to write five of them) until he was 47. He sent about half of the stanzas to *Fraser's Magazine*, but the editor sat on them and in the end did not publish any – no change in editorial practice there. In April 1859, in his 50th year, Fitzgerald published the poem at his own expense in an edition of 250 copies (24 pages at one shilling each). It sold badly and was finally sold off, two years later, at a penny a copy (again, no change there – this is called 'remaindering' and every poet knows about it). Dante Gabriel Rossetti found a copy in a second-hand bookshop and, as a result of his enthusiasm, another edition was published in 1868. Fitzgerald became at last (quite) famous, though never particularly rich. He spent the rest of his life tinkering with his stanzas and Tennyson came to tea: a happy ending of sorts.

Larkin did have a book of poems, *The North Ship*, published when he was at university, much to the (fairly) good-humoured exasperation and envy of his friend Kingsley Amis. But it wasn't a good book and it wasn't a good publisher; the good stuff didn't come out until 1955 when he was 33, and even then it wasn't from a *mainstream* publisher in London. Wendy Cope's *Making Cocoa for Kingsley Amis* came out when she was around 40, so there was actually a time when I was more famous, though we are more or less contemporary.

Gavin Ewart seems to belong in the other camp; he started very early, in his teens. But then there was a long hiatus after the War when he worked in advertising, and the section labelled 'Poems 1946–64' takes up just seven pages in a collected works that runs to nearly 900. It wasn't until he had been sacked – his word – by J Walter Thomson that he started again in the 1960s when he was approaching 50.

Another spot of autobiography

I did not write poems at school. The Royal High School in Edinburgh was not that kind of a place – though it counted Robert Fergusson, the man who showed Burns how to do it, and Walter Scott among its Former Pupils, as well as at least two contemporary poets (me and Tom Pow of *New Statesman* fame). Poems I wrote at university were so bad I never showed them to anyone. After six years in receipt of various grants I had to get a job. I taught foreign students and lived in a boarding house straight out of Balzac. Then I got a letter from Libby Purves (yes, the broadcaster, though she was a student then). She was editing, with the poet Sally Purcell, an anthology of poems by Oxford students to be called *The Happy Unicorns* and published by Sidgwick and Jackson. Could she use mine? She was short of laughs.

Didn't I say my poems were terrible? I did and they were. What Libby possessed were not *real* poems (I had a very high-minded idea of what real poems were); they were light verses about half a dozen in number and I had typed them onto the typewriter in her college room. She had a full social life and was never in when I called, so I sat at her typewriter and sent messages in verse, to which she replied, leaving her own efforts (I wonder what became of them) for the next time I came by. Thus she came into possession of a Whitworth oeuvre and after a time – for of course I accepted her invitation – *The Happy Unicorns* appeared and I got a cheque for five pounds signed by Lord Longford himself. The excellent Chris Reid is in the book too.

A published poet at twenty-something! For the next seven years I bombarded little magazines with poems, published – when I was published at all – in cyclostyled (a vile early version of copying) magazines with names like *Good Elf* and *Bogg*. I was *never* paid. In 1976 (I was 31) I got two poems into an Annual Arts Council Anthology called *New Poetry* – this was Number 2 – and I *was* paid and paid again in *New Poetry 3* and *4*. *New Poetry 4* was launched at the Chelsea Arts Club in 1978; all the contributing poets were invited. There must have been about 80 of us, paid for by your taxes; there was food (canapés on little cheesy biscuits) and big bottles of Italian wine. Poets roamed the floor with lapel badges; a wild-eyed beard was Anon. Anthony Thwaite, one of the editors, shook my hand, read my badge, exclaimed, 'So you're the one who writes the dirty poems! You're just as I imagined!' and disappeared. One poet passed out and had to be sent to Saint Pancras in a taxi. It was all agreeably bohemian. At chucking-out time the knot of poets I had attached myself to, which included the great Australian, Peter Porter, decided on to the nearest pub where I encountered Thwaite again and bought him a drink – one of the few career-enhancing moves I have ever consciously brought off. He enquired did I have any more poems. 'Why not send them to me now?' He was the poetry reader for Secker and Warburg and next day I sent off a sheaf of poems to

Secker, wondering what a poetry reader could possibly be.

It turned out to be (effectively at least) a poetry editor, and in a trice, well, in about two years, my first book appeared (1980), reviewed everywhere (poetry books were reviewed then) and winning a Poetry Society prize of £500. I was then 34 years old. Secker published two more books of mine; then Thwaite joined Andre Deutsch and the new broom swept me away. I found another publisher (after scarcely more than a year or two's frantic casting about): the excellent Harry Chambers, far from coincidentally one of the two judges who had awarded me that £500 prize – the UK poetry world is quite a small one.

Why am I telling you this – apart from the pleasure of boasting? I think to show that there is a certain amount of luck involved. I don't suppose Sidgwick and Jackson would have published a book of undergraduate verse from any university except Oxford (Lord Longford's university), so I was lucky to have gone there. Lucky too, to have met Libby Purves. Extremely lucky in the Thwaite business. Suppose I had drunk as much as the Old Lady of Leeds? Suppose I had not gone to that pub? Secker was exactly the right publisher for me then – I wasn't (perhaps) good enough for Faber; academic enough for OUP; Northern enough for Carcanet. Bloodaxe did not exist. So I was lucky.

On the other hand I *had* stuck at writing poems, pushing them into envelopes with sae and sending them off. I had stuck at it for ten years and got barely two dozen acceptances from respectable places (not *Bogg*, I mean). I had learned what I was good at and what I could not do. I knew that I had a talent for acrobatic rhyming, an ability to make people laugh and an agreeably sentimental streak. Also I knew a lot of poetry. In fact there wasn't a good English or Scots or Irish or Welsh poet from Chaucer to TS Eliot I hadn't read some of, though I was a bit sketchy on Americans and knew nothing at all about Australians, Canadians, New Zealanders, South Africans. I worked at my poetry, sat down in the evenings and wrote and rewrote, tried my hand at every form I could find. My favourite part of the business is actually still the *making* of poems; mild fame and little spurts of money (I earn a *living* from teaching) are agreeable bonuses. I think that is the way it has to be.

So what should you do?

Write some poems. And when you have written them, you should write them again – better. I once taught a man who said he didn't like to rewrite because he was afraid of losing the 'freshness' he found in Dylan Thomas. Now Thomas was a fanatical redrafter; more than 70 versions of one poem are extant. The only poet I have ever come across who didn't do this was Gavin Ewart, and I think he did the redrafting (like Doctor Johnson) in his head.

OK, you have written some poems. What now? *Read* some poems. Actually the reading should come first. You must, you really must, read what everybody else is doing, and what everybody else has done too, for the last few hundred years. Does that mean you should study English Literature at a university (as I did)? No it certainly doesn't, particularly these days when you will have to mug up lots of incomprehensible critical theory – a waste of time from your (poet's) point of view. You don't have to read *systematically* – you are a poet not a critic. But you must read.

Why read? To know *what has been done* and *what is being done*. If you don't know what has been done, then you are in danger of doing it again. And as for what is being done, if you don't know about that, then what yardstick have you to judge your own performance against? Even if you want to be a reactionary curmudgeon – Les Murray wrote a book of *Subhuman Redneck Poems*, and a very good book it is – then you do have to know what you are reacting *against*.

And when you read living poets, you may find that they are not quite as incomprehensible as you thought. You may find that they are fun. Is what you write at all like anything you have read? If it is not, then you might ask yourself why. Perhaps you are like Keats and will have to create the taste by which you are enjoyed. Perhaps you are like Shakespeare: he got his bad reviews too.

> An upstart crow beautified with our feathers that with his tiger's heart wrapped in a player's hide, supposes he is as well able to bumbast out a blank verse as the best of you, and being an absolute *Iohannes fac totum*, is in his own conceit the only Shake-scene in the country.

This is by Robert Greene, a fellow poet. Do not be too cast down by early lack of success; on the other hand, if there is *nobody else* writing like you, perhaps they all know something that you don't.

You've written your poems. You've read the opposition. You still think you have something to say. What do you do now? If you are a joiner, then you can join a group or sign up for a workshop.

Groups and workshops

> I went to a poetry workshop
> I worked on my poems a lot.
> When I read one out loud to the rest of the crowd
> Someone said it was good. It was not.
> > (quite encouraging though)

I went to a group years ago and I can't say I got a lot out of it. On the other hand I recently judged a competition open only to members of the Kent and Sussex Poetry Society and found the standard of writing high. Perhaps I am not a joiner, perhaps the group was wrong for me; you can't make hard-and-fast rules about this.

Poetry workshops? I run these, though again I never went to one when I was of an age for it to do me most good (too shy? too arrogant?). Wendy Cope confesses she was a workshop groupie and they helped her very much. I think her attitude is probably more useful to the emerging poet than mine. Of course the excellence, or otherwise, of the workshop depends very much upon the people who go to it and the poet(s) running it. Some use workshops as an ego-trip; they lay down the law and want to produce clones of themselves. If you feel that happening then throw your arms in the air, walk out and put it all down to experience. Most poets, I hope, are not like that and it can be very helpful to have your work criticised constructively – a good workshop will show you what is wrong (and what is right) and point the way to your further development. Last year I went to one for schoolchildren run by Matthew Sweeney – one of a team of poets recruited at a generous fee. Watching Sweeney putting over his ideas to huge young audiences helped to clarify some of my own. Years ago, when I was leading an Arvon workshop with another poet, I admired her ability to set a task and then *leave the poets alone* (where I would have been worrying at them). Poets have to be allowed to write their own poems and given the space to do so.

But in the end I do think that having a poem published in a respectable magazine will do you more good as a poet than a whole course of workshops. So how do you get published? Read on.

20. Getting your Poetry into Print

This is a shortened version of the article I update yearly for *Writers' and Artists' Yearbook*. You would do well to read what Peter Finch does for *The Writer's Handbook* – similar but not the same.

Poetry and money do not mix

Do not expect to make more than pin money directly from publication of your work. You may, in the fullness of time, make a tidy sum *indirectly* – I mean you get work because you are a published poet, you do readings, workshops, reviewing and so forth, if you like any of that sort of thing. But if you get £50 for a poem from a national magazine you may feel very satisfied, £40 or even £15 is more usual. As for your published volumes – they will not sell in four figures, nor do the publishers, except in a very few instances, expect them to. When OUP killed off their poetry list they said few sold 200 copies. I do a bit better than that – but then I would back Harry Chambers against all the big boys except Faber any day. In one sense nearly all poetry publishing is vanity publishing. Nobody is in it for the money.

What is vanity publishing?

Never give publishers money; that is what they give to you. Few poetry publishers make money from actually *selling* books. But those who ask authors to pay (usually a lot) for publication are known as Vanity Presses. They publish but they don't sell. They don't have to as their profit comes directly from you, the author. This is bad form. Getting money out of Arts Organisations (another phrase meaning the taxpayer) is, on the contrary, very good form, and most poetry publishers do it. Kingsley Amis famously thought all Arts subsidies were bad. But his poetry books always came from the publishers who were doing his fiction – Gollancz, then Cape, then Hutchinson – which is a subsidy, isn't it. And not all poets write popular novels, though Robert Graves and Cecil Day Lewis did, and John Harvey and Sophie Hannah do. A poet, whose name I can't remember, wrote one in *three days*!

Poetry editors

It does not do to have too much respect for the taste of individual literary editors. An editor is not God – whatever he (it usually is a he) thinks. Never forget that, though it can be hard if you are diffident – and most poets are (that's the ones who don't think they are Shakespeare and Superman rolled into one). But the fact that a particular bottom is warming an editorial chair may mean many things; it certainly does not mean papal infallibility. If Snooks of the Review sends back your work, despatch it immediately to Snurd of the Supplement. And if Snurd concurs with Snooks, they may both be wrong, indeed neither may actually have read (through or at all) what you sent, as Fiona Pitt-Kethley famously proved. Grit your teeth and send to Snarl and then to Snivel. Do not be discouraged by rejection – well of course you will be discouraged, but *try* not to be. If your poems are as good as you can make them and have been submitted in as professional a way as you can manage, then just keep on sending them out. I started writing poems in 1968, wrote my first good one in 1972, was paid my first proper money in 1976, and published a book in 1980. So patience and a thick skin are advantages.

It does help to have read the magazines. This will prevent you sending your bawdy ballad to *The Times Literary Supplement* or concrete poetry to *The Spectator*. But never forget the words of Charlie Coburn, the old music-hall entertainer. 'I sang my song to them, and they didn't like it. So I sang it again, and they still didn't like it. So I sang it a third time and one of them thought he might just get to like it if I changed the tune and altered the words. So I sang it again, just exactly the same way, and after a bit they all liked it.'

Submitting your work to magazines

I asked a number of poets about this. Some surprised me by saying
they never submitted to magazines at all; they waited to be asked.
I must say I think that a rather craven attitude, and if I waited like
that I would wait a very long time. But you can, I suppose, if you
are talented enough, carve out a poetic reputation through workshops and readings. In that case you must be good at putting yourself about in public and have the time and energy to expend on it.

All who did submit work regularly agreed on a number
of basics:

❑ Submit on A4 typed (single spacing is OK for poems) or printed
out from a word processor. One poet, David Phillips, reckoned
his percentage of successful submissions had gone up appreciably
since he bought his word processor, and he assumed it was
because his work now looked much more professional. It might
be, of course, that it has just got better.

❑ Make your submission look as professional as possible but
remember that the most professional layout won't save a duff
poem. Or I hope it won't, though when I think of you-know-
who and what's-his-name . . .

❑ Put your name and address at the bottom of each poem.
Editors, reasonably, do not keep your letters, only the poems
that interest them. You might consider a rubber stamp; I know
a number of poets who have them. There's a thing on my PC
that puts in addresses at the touch of a button!

❑ Fold the poem once and put it into the sort of envelope
designed to take A4 folded once. I don't know why poets like
to scrunch their verses into tiny envelopes, but don't do it.
Don't send it decorated in three colours of biro with admoni-
tions not to bend, etc.

❑ Include a stamped and self-addressed envelope of the same size.
This really is important. Shakespeare himself would be
consigned to the wpb without an appropriate sae.

❑ Do not send one poem. Do not send 20. Send enough to give a
reasonable flavour of your work – say about four or five. Long
poems are less likely to be accepted than short poems. If you
write different *kinds* of things, then make sure your selection
covers them. Send what you think of as your best work, but do
not be surprised if what is finally accepted is the one you put in

at the last minute, 'to make the others look better' as Larkin lugubriously puts it.

❏ If an editor says he likes your work and would like to see more, then send more as soon as possible. He wasn't being polite. Editors aren't. He said it because he meant it.

❏ Now is the time for some po-faced stuff about never sending the same poem to more than one editor simultaneously. As it happens, I don't do this much, but it appears that some well-known poets do. And indeed, if Snurd of the Supplement sits on your poems for six months, what are you supposed to do, since the polite follow-up letter recommended will, almost certainly, have no effect at all except to waste your time and your stamps? The real reason for not making multiple submissions is the embarrassment of having to make grovelling noises when the same poem is accepted by two editors simultaneously. I once, inadvertently, won two microscopic prizes in poetry competitions for the same poem. What did I do? I kept my mouth shut and cashed the cheques, that's what I did.

❏ You wouldn't have been daft enough to send off your only copies to Snurd, would you? Of course he lost them and it's all your own silly fault. No you can't sue him, but you'll know better next time. You can send photocopies and keep your originals. No, editors don't mind photocopies. Why should they?

❏ Keep your covering letter short, but if you have been published in reputable places, then it will do no harm to say so. This advice comes from Duncan Forbes. Selling poems is very like selling anything else, so blow your own trumpet, but don't blow for too long. Don't ask the editor for help in the advancement of your poetic career. He doesn't care, and anyway, what does he know? Being rude won't help either. I know artists are supposed to be rude and a lot of them are, too, but it hasn't actually helped them to anything except an ulcer or a punch on the nose.

Which magazines?

You could start with *The Times Literary Supplement* but I wouldn't advise it. One editor (not from the TLS) said honestly that he tended to reject, more or less unread, poems from anyone he had never heard of. Before you play with the big boys perhaps you ought to have some sort of a record in the little magazines. Some pay and some do not. The size of the cheque seems to depend on the size of the Arts Council grant rather than the quality of the magazine, though I suppose the two ought to have some sort of relationship. What matters is not the cash but whether you feel proud or ashamed to be seen in the thing. The Poetry Library at the South Bank Centre publishes a list of poetry magazines, and if you can get along there (very convenient for Waterloo Station and open seven days a week), you can nose around among the back numbers and see what is appealing to you. If you can't do that, then a letter with an sae will get you the list. The one I am looking at has well over 100 titles – from photo-copied and stapled compilations all the way up to *Poetry Review*, the magazine of the Poetry Society, to which I suggest you subscribe. There is also a list of American poetry magazines of which there are a great number. ('Anyone who cannot get poems published in America has simply run out of stamps.' Simon Rae.) Judge where you think you will fit in, and buy yourself a big sheet of second-class stamps. Send off your work and be prepared to be reasonably patient. Most editors reply in the end. Little magazines have a high mortality rate: be prepared for a particularly crushing form of disappointment – having your work accepted by a magazine which promptly ceases publication. It happens to us all. The Poetry Library also sends out, for an sae, a satisfying wodge of bumph about poetry publishing in general.

Some inexperienced poets seem worried that editors will filch their 'ideas' and pay them nothing. But poems are not made up of ideas; they are made up of words, and if anyone prints your words without permission they are infringing your copyright and you can threaten them with all sorts of horrible things. Honestly, this is a buyer's market, and even the editor of that smudgy rag has more material than he can use.

There is a new kind of organisation that solicits poems. Often with a name like Global or International, they don't ask for money up front, so they are not exactly Vanity Presses (*see* page 176), but encourage you – in lush marketers' prose – to buy anthologies for £40 or so. Harmless, I suppose, but you shouldn't have to pay for the magazine you are in; the publisher should send it to you free. Better to appear in something smaller along with poets you have actually heard of.

Poetry Review, the magazine of the Poetry Society, is quarterly, expensive and the best poetry magazine in the country. *Poetry Wales* and *New Welsh Review* are both beautifully produced, and though there is a certain amount of relentless celticity (why do celts do this?), other races can and do get poems printed in them. *Honest Ulsterman* is unpretentious but interesting and intelligent – you don't have to be at all Irish to contribute, either. *Ambit* is lively with good artwork; the editors take ages to look at submissions. *Stand* has gone international since the death of the old editor Jon Silkin, which seems all to the good. *London Magazine* is still excellent. *PN Review*, from Carcanet, is fierce critically and prints a wide range of poems. *Poetry London* is good and so is *The Rialto*, though in my opinion it could do with a beefier critical section. *Outposts* has been going for more than 50 years! This is a personal list – magazines I, in the South East of England, read from time to time. Check on what's local to you – local arts magazines, such as *Connections* down here in Kent, naturally lean towards local talent. Many more will be found in the National Poetry Library, the Northern Poetry Library and the Scottish Poetry Library.

The two literary heavyweights are *The Times Literary Supplement* and *The London Review of Books* who both publish poetry. *The Spectator* has restarted publishing poems, not often though. Poems appear from time to time in daily and Sunday newspapers; the fashion comes and goes. You can publish on the Internet. You won't get any money but readers can tell you what they think by email!

Book publication

Every poet wants to get a book out. How do you do it? One pretty sure way is to win a big prize in a competition – the National, the biennial Arvon, the Cardiff or Harry Chambers' Peterloo – though a high proportion of the winners have published books already, which seems unfair of them. Otherwise, you wait until you have reached the stage of having had two or three dozen poems published in reputable places. Then you type out enough poems for a collection – traditionally 64 pages (meaning 52 of poetry), but collections seem to be getting longer – and send them out, keeping your own copy and including return postage. I suppose that's what you do. I talked to Anthony Thwaite in a pub; everybody needs a slice of luck. I know excellent poets still trying to place their first book and, contrariwise, there are books from big publishers that are quite dreadful. Poetry, like most things, goes in fashions. Don't be in a hurry. Larkin's huge reputation rests on three books in a lifetime. Wait until you have some sort of a reputation in the magazines and small presses. Neil Astley at Bloodaxe reckons more than 90% of what comes through his letterbox he sends back, and he has usually had an eye on the successful ones before they got around to submitting.

Publishers

Faber are still out in front (though they did turn down Larkin's *The Less Deceived*, the most influential book of English poems in the last 50 years). It is not that their poets are all better, they are not, but Faber promote them and care about them. And being a Faber poet puts you in the company of Eliot and Larkin. Penguin have revived their Modern Poets series, but have not so far joined Faber on the railway bookstalls. Chatto, Cape and Picador do poetry (a bit); other big publishers are withdrawing (OUP, notoriously and shame on them) because poetry does not make them any money.

Being published by a household name does not mean selling thousands. Publishers like (or used to like) poetry on their list as a badge of virtue, but they don't want to know about it, they don't promote it and they don't persist with it. The book sinks or swims, and usually it sinks.

Specialist poetry presses – some, though not all of which, publish nothing but poetry – produce books that look every bit as good and, in most cases, sell every bit as well (or badly). Bloodaxe, Carcanet and Peterloo, none of them London-based, are leaders in the field.

Bloodaxe sounds fearsomely dismissive, but the name is from a Viking who conquered Northumberland. They have more titles and possibly better poets than Faber but they still fail the Railway Bookstall Test. 'From traditional formalists to post-modernists', says Neil Astley. Bloodaxe poets tend to be young and come from north of Watford. Carcanet have more titles than anyone else since Michael Schmidt shrewdly bought up the OUP list (for the permissions income, I guess); they publish Elizabeth Jennings, Les Murray, Sophie Hannah and John Ashbery, which indicates Schmidt's catholicity and willingness to go outside this country. He sees them as 'extending the Wordsworthian tradition of the common voice' and welcomes manuscripts, though he wishes people would read (and buy presumably) some of the books on his list first. This is good advice; every publisher has a style, just as every magazine has. Peterloo picks up older poets who have been unjustly overlooked. He first published Kirkpatrick Dobie in that poet's 84th year. Dana Gioia, the American 'new formalist' and Ursula Fanthorpe, the one *The Guardian* tipped for Laureate, are his biggest guns.

Anvil is London-based and does a lot of poetry in translation. Enitharmon's books are as well produced as anyone's: it's a good list (Anthony Thwaite, Vernon Scannell, Duncan Forbes), unfashionable and none the worse for that, with some beautiful artwork. There are some interesting new(ish) names. Leviathan is Michael Hulse, poet-editor of *Stand*; he snapped up Kit Wright from Hutchinson who shamefully allowed his poetry to go out of print. Blackwater Press (not to be confused with Blackstaff which is Irish) has an expanding list. Headland is the indefatigable Gladys Mary Coles.

Most are represented by Signature, a distribution network working for small literary presses (mostly, but not exclusively, poetry) in the UK and Eire. It has its own warehouse and deals with the Jiffy-bagging of books to bookshops and individual customers for most – though not all – of its members. It is expanding into Europe, with agencies in many EU countries. If this system works well, then there is little advantage to be gained from going with the big publishers. Except Faber of course.

Getting on radio

Michael Conaghan, who has had many poems broadcast, writes: 'BBC local radio – more talk than its commercial equivalent – is the place to start. Find out those responsible for Arts programming and contact them. Short, punchy, topical work is probably what they want, and Events/Festivals concentrate their minds wonderfully.'

Poetry on the Internet

The poet Peter Howard writes an Internet column for *Poetry Review*. He says, 'You'll need a computer (PC or Mac) a modem and a phone line. Any of the service providers are eager to give you an Internet connection for nothing. Then you can email and surf the Web. Submit to electronic magazines or set up your own site and get people to visit it. Set up your own magazine – there's no extra charge. Everything's up for grabs – there are no real reputations yet, though they're forming.'

Competitions

Some poets are snooty about these. Of course they are popular because they can make money for the organisers. Think of the numbers: a *big* competition *may* attract 8000 entries paying (say) £4 a time. That gives an income of £32,000, enough to pay for some good prizes, a fair bit of promotion, fees for the judges and running costs, and still leave a nice bit in the kitty. But, from the poet's end, it is a good deal too. Over the last ten years I have entered numerous competitions. I haven't won any of the big ones (though I did get a second in the Peterloo) but I've won enough prizes from £1000 down to £25 to come out on the right side of the ledger. Others have done much better. Simon Rae has won the National and been second twice, so how does he do it – beyond just writing very good poems? And though unknowns (everybody starts as an unknown, don't they?) only occasionally win the big prizes, they do pick up the smaller ones quite often, and that can be a great encouragement when you need it. Competitions – and I have judged plenty – are organised fairly in my experience. Everyone does have an equal chance and though light verse rarely wins, it does get lesser prizes. Don't forget *The Spectator*'s competitions set by Jaspistos (the poet James Mitchie). You can win £20 and a bottle of Scotch by doing something like the exercises in this book. I have. Members of my Creative Writing classes have.

Some competitions offer pamphlet publication as a prize. You submit a bunch of poems and an increased entry fee (£10 or so). There doesn't seem anything wrong with this, though you obviously shouldn't try before you have a good number of poems you feel proud of. Most poets started with pamphlet publication.

Self-publishing

If you want your work in print and nobody will do it for you without a cheque, do it yourself. Blake did. And Jorge Luis Borges, who distributed copies by stuffing them into the pockets of literary men's overcoats. Peter Finch has written an excellent book on this and there is a paper you can buy from the Society of Authors (free to members).

Getting paid

Since I like writing poems, getting paid seems a bonus. But try not to think that way. There are plenty of people (organisers of Festivals and whatnot) who will try to get your services and your work for next-to-nothing or even nothing. Of course it is up to you whether you accept, and some sort of exposure may be worth having. But if there is money about – and often there is – make sure you get a share. Don't be shy about asking. I have done a poetry reading to a handful of people for £175 (my usual whack is £100), and Carol Ann Duffy can command three times that. When I wrote poems for *The Independent* a few years back I was getting £200 plus per poem – and why not! Poetry magazines don't pay anything like that, often all you get is a free copy, but newspapers are awash with money. A published poet should get £100 for a couple of hours in a school and £200 for a whole day. A good rule is to get what you can without appearing too grasping. Most poets are not good with money. I'm not good with money. *Don't leave a venue without the cheque*! I have twice had to wait while they rustled up a cheque-signer from a distant living room. However, I will say that my poetry cheques have never yet bounced.

21. Books to Read

There are books you really ought to have, at least according to me; for you cannot do your poet's job without them. There are others that are interesting and instructive. I have put the first category in **heavy type** and the second in *italics*. There is a third category of books that should be burned immediately (again according to me) and a fourth of books I haven't read. Neither of these is represented below.

Dictionaries

Since poems are made out of words, foremost among these is a good dictionary. I have **The Shorter Oxford Dictionary** and the Complete Oxford (the one with the magnifying glass). I used to have *The Concise Oxford Dictionary* until my daughter carried it away to the devastation that is her bedroom. I miss it; I think everyone needs something comprehensive, one of the big Oxfords, and something in one volume. *Chambers* is good for crossword solvers, if you happen to be one of those. *Webster's* is American (of course) and better in some ways, my wife tells me – she has one. I have **Roget's Thesaurus**, and so should you (I am on my second copy). I also have the **Penguin Rhyming Dictionary**; some poets turn their free-verse noses up at rhyming dictionaries, but Byron didn't (he used Walker's which is no longer available). Of course a rhyming dictionary won't help you with the off-rhymes, or it won't until you become fairly adept at using it. *The Poet's Manual and Rhyming Dictionary* by Frances Stillman has the advantage of giving you two books for the price of one. Looking upon my shelves I also have a Dictionary of Anagrams, a Crossword Dictionary, three Dictionaries of Slang (one is American), a Scots Dictionary and a Dictionary of Idioms, designed for foreign students, all of which I have used in writing poems.

Books about language

Don't mess about. Save up your pennies and buy the best. When you win a £20 book token prize for a poem, spend it all on David Crystal's **Cambridge Dictionary of the English Language**. I think every poet ought to spend time with this marvellous book; how can you say you are a poet if you do not know about, and have no interest in, the material you are working with? English is surely the finest language the world has ever seen for comprehensiveness, inventiveness, exuberance and just about everything else I can think of. Pity the French, who, like the Romans before them, have to make do with a small, if elegant, vocabulary (that's why they keep on borrowing ours); and the Scots Gaels, who have a language of unparalleled mellifluousness and but a handful of people left to speak it. Treasure your heritage; it is the language itself that writes the best bits of your poems. Crystal's other books are worth looking at too, particularly his *Language Play* (Penguin) about the ludic element I touched on earlier. I have *Fowler's Modern English Usage* and Eric Partridge's Usage and Abusage, neither of which is particularly modern any more.

Poetic terminology and poetic forms

The Princeton Handbook of Poetic Terms edited by Alex Preminger needs to be ordered, since it is published in the US, but it has the sterling American virtues of thoroughness and cheapness (under £10 when I bought it). I have a number of those Methuen Critical Idiom books: *The Stanza* by Ernst Haublein; *Metre Rhyme and Free Verse* by GS Fraser and *The Sonnet* by John Fuller, which is a little gem, though rather costly at only 50 pages long. *Metre, Rhythm and Verse Form* (Routledge) by the poet Philip Hobsbaum is very good. **Rhyme's Reason** (Yale), which he subtitles 'A Guide to English Verse', by the poet John Hollander is (perhaps) the best of all; if you want to know how a pantoum is structured then Hollander will not only *tell* you (Preminger does that), but *show* you with an example of his own. *How to be Well-Versed in Poetry* (Penguin) edited by EO Parrott does something similar, using a squad of Literary Competition winners. It will not replace Hollander, but it's funny and quite cheap.

Poets on poetry

Good poets often, though not always, have good things to say about poetry. The list could be as long as a pretty fair-sized piece of string, but these are my top five: WH Auden's *The Dyer's Hand*, Robert Graves' *The Crowning Privilege* (though be warned – he puts the boot into *all* his contemporaries), Louis MacNeice's *The Strings Are False* (an unfinished autobiography) and Philip Larkin's *Required Writing* are all worth reading and re-reading, and Les Murray's *The Paperbark Tree*, a splendid new boy on my shelves. Seamus Heaney and Ted Hughes are always worth listening to. Americans William Carlos Williams and Robert Frost are good (particularly Carlos Williams). Wallace Stevens likes gnomic aphorisms. Read Ezra Pound's *ABC of Reading* if you can stand his *enfant terrible* hectoring tone – battles fought a long time ago with Pound generally on the winning side (except in Hitler's War, of course). **The Practice of Poetry: Writing Exercises from Poets Who Teach** (Harper Perennial) edited by Robin Behn and Chase Twichell is just what it says. *In the Palm of Your Hand* (Tilbury) by Steve Kowit is engaging and instructive, though he has not heard of the UK poetwise. These are both American of course, for in the US every campus has its resident creative writing poet.

Non-poets on poetry

I have an excellent book **The Poet's Craft** (CUP) by AF Scott, which looks at poets' manuscripts, printed revisions and sources. *Poems in Progress* by Phyllis Bartlett (OUP) covers similar ground. Both may well be – almost certainly are – out of print but worth looking for. *Poetic Meter & Poetic Form* by Paul Fussell (Random House) was not written, the author insists, 'to teach aspiring writers to produce passable verses', but it will do just that. Witty, acerbic and learned.

How-to-write-poetry books

There are quite a lot of these and the quality is variable. *Writing Poetry and Getting It Published* by Matthew Sweeney and John Hartley Williams is good – but don't take all the authors' prejudices, frankly expressed, too seriously. Don't take my prejudices too seriously either. *Writing Poems* by Peter Sansom (too short) and

The Way To Write Poetry by Michael Baldwin both have their moments. *Getting Into Poetry* by Paul Hyland is not about writing poetry at all, more about 'the scene'. A good jaunty and instructive read, and how could I respond less than warmly to someone who calls me 'the Light Verse hard man' (though that's not me, Paul, I'm an old softy – the Light Verse hard person must be Carol Ann Duffy). *How To Publish Your Poetry* by Peter Finch is just what it says, a handbook about self-publication from someone who knows.

Finch writes the article on poetry in *The Writer's Handbook* and I do it in *Writer's and Artist's Yearbook*. You ought to have one of these (you don't really need both) and make sure it is no more than about three years old – information about publishers and publications changes fairly fast.

General anthologies of poetry

If you want a general Anthology of English Poetry there are plenty on offer. I should buy the fattest one you can find. You will probably find it in a second-hand shop. Helen Gardner's *Oxford Anthology of English Verse* is good.

20th century anthologies of poetry

The two I like best are *The Oxford Book of Twentieth Century Verse* edited by Philip Larkin (except of course that it isn't, since he did it 20 years before the end of the century) and **Scanning The Century** edited by Peter Forbes (Viking/Penguin). Both of these have a very wide selection and a lot of pages, giving you more poems for your money. *The Oxford Book of Contemporary Verse (1945–1980)* edited by DJ Enright is good too, though again it doesn't cover the last 20 years.

Anthologies of light verse

These are good for two reasons: they are funny and full of inventive verse forms. I continue to enjoy Gavin Ewart's **The Penguin Book of Light Verse** and Kingsley Amis' *The Oxford Book of Light Verse*. Ewart gives you more bang for your bucks but why not have both? If you can find any of JM Cohen's anthologies of

Comic and Curious Verse (Penguin) second hand, then snap them up. Wendy Cope's *The Funny Side* (Faber) is short, but it contains poems I have not seen elsewhere and it certainly makes me laugh.

Anthologies for children

I know you are not a child but you might have some – or nephews, nieces, etc. who get Christmas presents. Avoid those little paperbacks with names like 'Poems about Snot' – but I'm sure you would anyway. *The Ring of Words* edited by Roger McGough (Faber) is a wonderful book, and *The Kingfisher Book of Comic Verse*, also edited by Roger McGough is funny and contains lots of poems I hadn't seen before.

A special category

I must mention Anthony Burgess' Enderby novels, particularly the original trilogy. They spurred me on when I was younger, and Enderby, the poet who composes only in the lavatory, is the genuine article.

Appendix 1

I used 'The Sleepout' by Les Murray in a writing exercise described in *The Practice of Poetry*. We worked from a triple-spaced text and 'translated' the poem line by line. Then we rewrote, removing the scaffolding of the original poem. The success of such an exercise probably depends quite a lot on that original and I tried to choose a poem whose subject was accessible to most people – like the look of your bedroom when you were a small child.

The Sleepout

Childhood sleeps in a verandah room
in an iron bed close to the wall
where the winter over the railing
swelled the blind on its timber boom

and splinters picked lint off warm linen
and the stars were out over the hill;
then one wall of the room was forest
and all things in there were to come.

Breathings climbed up on the verandah
when dark cattle rubbed at a corner
and sometimes dim towering rain stood
for forest, and the dry cave hunched woollen.

Inside the forest was lamplit
along tracks to a starry creek bed
and beyond lay the never-fenced country,
its full billabongs all surrounded

by animals and birds in loud crustings,
And something kept leaping up amongst them.
And out there, to kindle whenever
dark found it, hung the daylight moon.

The Artist

The only child sleeps in a tall high room
in an army bed somebody had
and painted with crocus and daffodil paint
in a bright random manner called stippling

and the walls were all pink new distemper
with a frieze of old picture book scraps
and the chair by the bed which was shiny dark green
held a standard lamp made from German shells

with the flex with the switch near the pillow
so that men with great axes and circular saws
could be quickly and easily illuminated
and the lamp was part painted with cream and tan paint

and the other part all tan and cream
and tastefully stippled, not just flat and plain.
It must have been his favourite combination
there were some shy excursions into orange

and dark brown which didn't quite please him
and I guess West Ken was different then when
I was badly timed and we were kind
and refined and stippled all our things

The White House

High up under the eaves he slept
in his attic room, far, far from his brothers,
where frost had frozen the window shut
and cracked the glass at its four corners.

Sun rose over the London Midland & Scottish Railway:
the meccano and Loppylugs were warm in the bed beside him
and the white ceiling was stained with islands
and the islands stretched out for ever and ever.

Some nights you could hear the whole house breathing
and a tap-tap-tapping in the wainscot
that was rats, that was fat black rats
scratching and sniffing and snuffling for a way in

except there was no way, no way in,
not for the rats, not for the white screech owls
beating with their great white wings at the window,
not for the white wolves nor the were-wolves,

191

Nor the lurkers in their fluttering coats,
As they lurked and they lounged and they sang high how
the gods of the LMS and the gods of meccano
and the gods of sweet sucked soft toys were ailing, ailing.

The Why Child

The why child wakes in the cold attic,
where the white moon plays silver tricks
with ferret faces in frosty windows
and burrowing danger scatters fear

over the oak beamed walls, like flurries
of snow blurring the edge of what is,
until the frozen window panes
become wet with the ferret's breathings.

The waking nightmare that follows
rips open the white gown of sleep.
And the sharp-tooth taste of tomorrow
is the curdled milk of bad dreams.

The why child is awake in the attic,
afraid of the white daylight moon,
afraid of the ferret familiar
that eats up the long afternoon.

You might feel that this sort of thing is like copying from your
neighbour at school. To me it is no more than using a form (like
the sonnet form) to say something that is your own. The three
poems modelled on Les Murray's are, in order, by Janet Bailey,
John Whitworth and June English. You will no doubt have
noticed that June English's poem – perhaps the best of the three –
has lost a stanza somewhere in the redrafting stages and moves
from four-beat lines like Murrays to three-beat lines at the
midpoint.

Appendix 2

Simon Rae wins competitions and writes occasional verse for *The Guardian*. The poem below stands here as a representative of the sort of poetry written nowadays that I like. It is in metrical form (iambic tetrameter triplets) with rhymes (though not to a set pattern) as well as most of the near-rhymes we talked about. It does not capitalise at the beginning of the line. The language is emphatically the way we speak now ('one had wheels', 'soundtracked', 'slo-mo') and not at all obscure: though I confess I don't know what baler twine is, beyond string. There are similes and metaphors, but the poem isn't jampacked with them. It tells a story which sounds to me – I don't know and Rae doesn't tell us – like something you might read in a newspaper. It does not preach, a fault in many 'amateur' poems; it has no encapsulated message, though there is certainly a 'meaning' to be found – something to do with ideas of maleness and courage I should say. Many, though not all, of its merits are those of good writing, rather than poetry in particular. It is unusual in being 48 lines long – I tend to keep my poems down to the 40 which is the limit for so many poetry competitions.

The Boys in the Barn

One had wheels and one knew the barn
and the third palmed his sister's portable phone,
a place, a time, and the job was done.

The pick up was easy, the back seat giggly,
the driving a little bit higgledy-piggledy.
They drove through the dusk and just missed an owl

or the owl missed them, filling the windscreen
with its outspread cope, its incredible wing-span,
and veered off the radar into the hedgerow

soundtracked by screams and a half-hearted jeer.
The baler twine didn't give them much trouble
and the doors scraped back untombing a darkness

as warm as a duvet, a warehouse stacked
as high as the roof with the scent of hay.
they trampolined in and yodelled a bit,

then spread their jackets and turned out pockets
for tablets and packets and passed round the cider
and shared a bad joke and laughed too loud.

and after – well, they were back in the crowd.
It was one of those times when everyone smokes:
the sense of triumph, the ease, the booze...

And which of them came first to his senses
and furnished a name for what he noticed
is not recorded, but he raised the alarm

and they felt the panic rising like vomit
as arms were forced into apple-pie sleeves
and legs bent crooked and shoes went missing

in a slo-mo nightmare of kicking and shouting
and giving directions and buckling belts
and choking and coughing and stamping until

out in the air they could breathe they stood
in their scarecrow shirts and guyfawkes trousers
slapping their sides and feeling their hair.

They looked up at the sightscreens of fire
and the flames ate their cries and they covered their faces.
This was a crisis that couldn't be sorted

with a laugh and a fag and a blast of Oasis.
And what it said about dates and destiny
and the role of the hero could be worked out later.

A beam collapsed and the heat grew greater.
Then the doors fell out and the roof caved in
which seemed to be freighted with a certain meaning.

They decided it might look less bad in the morning,
and who had the car keys (who the *fuck*
had the car keys?) and what was that siren?

They were young, and had much to learn.
So they turned their backs on the barn, leaving
their first loves, if such they were, to burn.

Index

Index to Exercises

Acknowledgements

Auden, WH: *Twelve Songs IX* taken from 'Collected Poems'. Reproduced by permission of Faber & Faber Ltd. Published by Faber & Faber Ltd, London.

Bartlett, Phyllis: Extract taken from 'Poets in Process'. © Phyllis Bartlett. Reproduced by permission of Oxford University Press.

Berryman, John: Excerpt taken from *Dream Song # 22 of 1826* from '77 Dream Songs'. Copyright © 1964 by John Berryman. Copyright renewed 1992 by Kate Berryman. Reproduced by permission of Faber & Faber Ltd. Published by Faber & Faber Ltd, London. Reproduced in North America by permission of Farrar, Straus and Giroux, LLC.

Betjeman, John: Extract taken from 'Summoned by Bells'. Reproduced by permission of John Murray (Publishers) Ltd.

Causely, Charles: *Guy Fawkes Day* taken from 'Collected Poems'. Reproduced by permission of David Higham Associates on behalf of Macmillan.

Chesterton, GK: Extract taken from 'The Scandal of Father Brown'. Reproduced by permission of A.P. Watt on behalf of The Royal Literary Fund.

Cummings, EE: 'the one and only thing that mattered about a poem was what it said' is reprinted from SIX NON LECTURES, 1953, by permission of WW Norton & Co. Copyright © 1999 by the trustees for

Acknowledgements

the EE Cummings trust and George James Firmage. 'l(a' is reprinted from COMPLETE POEMS 1904-1962, by EE Cummings, edited by George James Firmage, by permission of WW Norton & Co. Copyright © 1991 by the Trustees for the EE Cummings Trust and George James Firmage.

Drysdale, Ann: *Gay Science* taken from 'Villanelle for Two Friends'. © Ann Drysdale 1999. Reproduced by permission of Peterloo Poets.

Eliot, TS: Extract taken from *The Waste Land*. Reproduced by permission of Faber & Faber Ltd. Published by Faber & Faber Ltd, London.

Ewart, Gavin: Extracts taken from 'Collected Poems'. Reproduced by permission of Margo Ewart.

Fanthorpe, UA: *Riddle* taken from 'The New Exeter Book of Riddles' (1999). Reproduced by permission of Enitharmon Press.

Frame, Janet: Extract taken from 'Janet Frame: An Autobiography'. Reprinted by permission of The Women's Press.

Graves, Robert: Extracts taken from several poems published in 'Complete Poems'. Reproduced by permission of Carcanet Press.

Hannah, Sophie: *Ghazal* taken from 'Hero and the Girl Next Door'. Reproduced by permission of Carcanet Press.

Heaney, Seamus: *The Forge* taken from 'Opened Ground'. Reproduced by permission of Faber & Faber Ltd. Published by Faber & Faber Ltd, London.

Heath-Stubbs, John: Extract taken from 'Collected Poems 1943–1987'. Reproduced by permission of David Higham Associates on behalf of Carcanet Press.

Howard, Peter: *Enthusiastic Echolalia* reproduced by permission of Peter Howard.

Hughes, Ted: Extract taken from *Winter Pollen*. Reproduced by permission of Faber & Faber Ltd. Published by Faber & Faber Ltd, London.

Jakowska, Nicki: *Conservaratory for Ladies of Pleasure* taken from 'Lighting a Slow Fuse' (1998). Reproduced by permission of Enitharmon Press.

Kipling,Rudyard: Detail taken from *Mandalay*. Reproduced by permission of AP Watt Ltd on behalf of the National Trust for Places of Historical Interest or Natural Beauty.

Larkin, Philip: Extracts taken from 'Required Writing' and *The Explosion* taken from 'Collected Poems'. © 1983 by Philip Larkin.Reproduced by permission of Faber & Faber Ltd. Published by Faber & Faber Ltd, London. Reproduced in the United States by permission of Farrar, Straus and Giroux, LLC.

Leonard, Tom: *Feed ma Lamz* taken from 'Intimate Voices'. Reproduced by permission of the author.

MacNeice, Louis: Bagpipe Music taken from 'Collected Poems'. Published by Faber & Faber. Reproduced by permission of David Higham Associates..

McGough, Roger: *Laughing All the Way to the Bank*. Reprinted by permission of PFD on behalf of Roger McGough. © Roger McGough: as printed in the original volume.

Murray, Les: *The Sleepout* and detail taken from 'The Paperbark Tree'. Reproduced by permission of Carcanet Press.

Pound, Ezra: Extract taken from 'Selected Prose'. Reproduced by permission of Faber & Faber Ltd. Published by Faber & Faber Ltd, London.

Reading, Peter: *Perduta Gente* taken from 'Collected Poems 2: Poems 1985–1996' (1996). Reproduced by permission of Bloodaxe Books.

Stevens, Wallace: Extract taken from 'Collected Poems'. Reproduced by permission of Faber & Faber Ltd. Published by Faber & Faber Ltd, London.

Williams, William Carlos: Detail taken from 'Collected Poems'. Reproduced by permission of Carcanet Press.

Wright, Kit: *George Herbert's Other Self in Africa* taken from 'Hoping it Might be So', published in 2000 by Leviathan.

Yeats, WB: Extracts taken from 'Collected Poems'. Reproduced by permission of A.P. Watt on behalf of Michael B. Yeats. Reprinted with the permission of Scribner, a Division of Simon & Schuster, Inc., from THE COLLECTED WORKS OF WB YEATS, VOLUME 1: THE POEMS, REVISED, edited by Richards J Finneran. (New York: Scribner 1997).

Every effort has been made to trace and acknowledge copyright owners. If any right has been omitted the publishers offer their apologies and will rectify this in subsequent editions following notification.